by Aram Saroyan

POETRY

Aram Saroyan (1968)
Pages (1969)
Words & Photographs (1970)
Cloth: An Electric Novel (1971)
The Rest (1971)
Poems (1972)
O My Generation and Other Poems (1976)
Day and Night: Bolinas Poems (1998)

PROSE

The Street: An Autobiographical Novel (1974)
*Genesis Angels: The Saga of Lew Welch and
the Beat Generation* (1979)
Last Rites: The Death of William Saroyan (1982)
William Saroyan (1983)
Trio: Portrait of an Intimate Friendship (1985)
The Romantic (1988)
*Friends in the World: The Education of a Writer:
A Memoir* (1992)
*Rancho Mirage: An American Tragedy of
Manners, Madness, and Murder* (1993)

EDITOR

Selected Poems by Archie Minasian (1986)
Selected Poems by Ted Berrigan (1994)

ARAM SAROYAN

DAY & NIGHT

BOLINAS POEMS

BLACK SPARROW PRESS

SANTA ROSA · 1998

ACKNOWLEDGMENTS

Grateful acknowledgement is made to the editors and publishers of the following publications, in which some of these poems first appeared: *American Poetry Review, Ararat, Beaulines, Best Poems of 1974: Borestone Mountain Poetry Awards, Big Sky, Blasts, Bobo: A Collection of Bolinas Writing, The Bolinas Hearsay News, Buffalo Stamps, Chicago, City Paper* (Baltimore), *Coldspring Journal, Contact, DeKalb Literary Arts Journal, The Ear* (Australia), *The End, Fallow Deer, Floating Island, The Human Handkerchief* (U.K.), *Hye Cherzoom, I Sing the Song of Myself* (Greenwillow, 1978), *L, Lip, The Lodestar Broadsides, The Milk Quarterly, The Nation, New Age Journal, New Directions 33* (New Directions, 1976), *The New York Times Sunday Magazine, Nomad, Oculist Witnesses, 100 Posters, Out There, The Paris Review, The Poet Exposed* (Van de Marck, 1986), *Poetry: A Magazine of Verse* ("Life Is No Arrival" and "Life Is a Dream"), *Poetry Review* (U.K.), *Rolling Stone, The San Francisco Examiner, Sotto Voce* (U.K.), *10 California Poets, The Trinity Times, The Turkey Buzzard Review* and *The Village Voice.*

LIBRARY OF CONGRESS CATALOGING-IN-PUBLICATION DATA

Saroyan, Aram
    Day and night: Bolinas poems / Aram Saroyan.
      p.   cm.
    ISBN 1-57423-085-9 (paperback)
    ISBN 1-57423-086-7 (cloth trade)
    ISBN 1-57423-087-5 (signed cloth)
      I. Bolinas (Calif.)—Poetry. 2. Autobiography—Poetry.
I. Title.
PS3569.A72D39   1998   98-37108
811'.54—dc21   CIP

CONTENTS

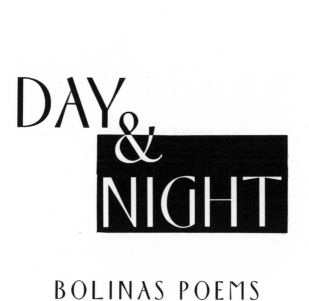

DAY & NIGHT

BOLINAS POEMS

To the Town Itself

There Are Animals in This Area

LINES FOR MY AUTOBIOGRAPHY

To Gailyn

I

I put the food on my sister's plate.
I wished that I could stay up late.
I talked out of turn in class.
I begged Mrs. Donovan not to send me to the principal.
My father met me on the stairs and said sternly,
"Good morning, Aram."

I fell down the stairs.
I pumped up the wheel of my bicycle.
I ate Rice Krispies for breakfast.
I hit the bull's-eye
I flew the kite.
I went out to play baseball.

I liked a girl named Jill Salisbury.
She had a great complexion and black hair.
She looked like a picture of health.
She looked beautiful.
She looked like she had a good heart and spirit.
My mother moved my sister and me to New York.

The lights of Times Square amazed me.
I had never seen so many lights before.
So many different colors.
My friends were different here.
Jimmy Peck collected Benny Goodman records.
I started taking pictures.

I started talking to the mirror.
I thought I could sing.

I read *The Catcher in the Rye* twice.
I no longer talked with my sister.
My life became introspective.
I went to movies and art galleries.
I began to masturbate.

Tits.
I thought about tits all day.
Tits laid heavy on my thoughts.
Tits took over my thoughts.
My only thoughts were tits.
Tits looked at me out of the pages of girlie magazines
And I looked back.

I saw my mother's tits.
I saw my sister's tits.
I saw my grandmother's tits.
I saw a lady-in-a-window's tits.
They seemed quite large.
I wondered how large they were if you were in the room.

I thought about climbing in her window.
I met Diana.
We hung around together with Jerry.
Jerry was in love with her.
We humped everywhere.
I felt her tits.

I worried that I was stupid.
I worried that I never read books.
I thought I was worthless.
I knew I had a low I.Q.
I wondered about fucking.
I knew nothing.

I couldn't fuck.

I masturbated without an erection.
I looked at my penis.
I decided to retire from public life.
I wondered if I was gay.
I read *Naked Lunch* wondering if I'd get a hardon.

Steve and I lived together in a room
A few steps under the sidewalk.
We *tied* the refrigerator shut.
I slept on an army cot.
My shoes were too tight.
Steve sat on his bed, thinking.

I worked as a messenger.
The summer was hot.
I went to the University of Chicago.
Chicago was below zero.
My roommate read a new book of poetry every night.
I thought he was healthy.

I knew I was sick.
I felt relieved to know it.
I dropped out.
I went back to New York.
I hung around with Joe and Harvey.
Joe liked Bob Dylan early.

I looked at my hand.
I looked at my hand.
I wrote some poems.
I felt calm somehow.
I thought I ought to be
What I knew I was.

Adolescence is heady.
Adolescence is dull.

Adolescence is a long time
To be so ugly.
Adolescence is awful.
Adolescence is full.

II

I recognized you the minute I saw you.
I liked being with you.
You amaze me.
I love you.
You and I look alike.
I feel like I feel like you do.

You are beautiful.
The things you do.
You remind me of a flower.
And a swan.
But you are you.
You make me feel Persian.

The lion in me answers the lion in you.
We go together well.
I like walking with you.
We have the same speed even though we are different.
You know me well.
You are a part of my nature.

My life with you is a poem
You and I write together
Every day by hand
Until we are no longer writing it
It just seems to write itself
Like having a baby

I love you and the little one.
Little is what she is.
Cute little shoes.
Delicate little dogs.
A little thomas hardy.
Anything you care to name, little.

She reminds me of little things.
She seems so clean in her ways.
She is so happy.
What a little girl.
This little girl is
One of the most beautiful little girls in the world.

She knows what she wants
And she wants what she knows
She knows what she wants
And she wants what she knows
She knows what she wants
And she wants what she knows

Eye
Nose
Mouth
Ear
Hair
She says

We knew what we were doing
When we made her.
We know even better.
We know even better.
You are so beautiful.
You're so beautiful.

You remind me of you.

I see you in every way.
Hello.
I love you.
Hello.
I love you.

Sex is so great with you.
Sex is so
Great with you.
Sex is
So great with you.
Sex is so great with you.

Your tits in my mouth.
Your mouth in my mouth.
My cock in your pussy.
Your pussy in my cock.
I like you a lot.
Wet.

III

The life of a poet is hard.
Strangely athletic.
Practicing feats of endurance in New York City.
There may be no money.
People come and go casually through the streets
So long as they are not empty-handed.

Humility is magnetic.
People are friendly.
You are there
In naked air, no possessions—living in The Chelsea
With Gailyn.
"Hello, people." (Leonard Cohen)

You wish Larry loved you.
You wish Tom loved you too.
Everybody should love you.
You great poet.
You eagle
Of literature.

We went out today around three.
Strawberry walked behind me
While I walked thinking about this poem.
Then I turned to her.
She had just woken up from her nap.
She was still half-asleep.

A slow Sunday.
You sew.
I think about poetry.
Tom comes by.
Hi, Tom.
Then he goes away again.

Time goes by so slowly.
The rocks on the beach keep up the beat.
Chuck Berry is still a genius.
Picasso remains invisible.
Poets are paid one dollar a line by *Poetry*.
$1.00.

Who will buy my new poem?
It's a wristwatch in a new way.
Don't worry.
It's really good.
I speak Italian.
Believe me.

You do.

I do, too.
Soon, everybody.
Soon, *The New York Review of Books,*
Playboy,
TV.

I won't sign anything.
I'll just let it be me.
I'm ready to step on the gas.
I'll release the screen rights.
Anyone can have a piece of me.
I'm all heart, solid gold.

A lot of people have been teaching me.
I've learned from experience too.
Influences?
There are a lot of them.
Too many to name.
I'm hunting something.

Or maybe I'm being hunted.
The rainbow sleeping at the end of every day.
The hour of grace after the dinner table.
The noise of something moving in the room.
It's cold in here.
Quick, light a fire.

I know nothing about fire.
I know everything about fire.
I know everything
And I know nothing,
Everything and nothing,
About fire.

What is this?
What is this night?

What is this night I'm in?
The cat comes up
To be patted.
I'm half-asleep already.

Pick up a rock
In a dream
And look at it
For what it is,
A piece of time.
The life of a poet is beautiful.

FOR TOM CLARK

Big city boys come out
to the country, toy with

the idea
of becoming farmers, forgetting

their nervous systems for a while,
it almost seems easy (why

write poetry about dock strikes?)—
their wives cooperate with

nature so well, or seem to know
their own rhythm better

than men, creatures of crude habit
perhaps, an Orange Julius might hit

the spot
right now—they think, circling and

circling the precise matter of their own
home, and children come into this

as quickly as they find themselves
a place in it, meanwhile the planet spins

and keeps time perfectly with the Universe
like a guitar solo by Eric

Clapton (Derek & The Dominoes) it all
seems to fit, nothing impressionably wrong

or jarringly accurate, even—that too
becoming useless as we go on in this life,

soon to hit thirty, soon to hit twenty-nine,
and getting better and better all the time.

MY MOTHER AND MY FATHER

My mother has it in her.
My father has it in him, too.
But neither of them found it for long
In each other, marrying and divorcing
Twice by the time I was eight.

From that time on, I sided with my mother I'd say.
That is, I lived with her
And my father visited. Or Lucy and I
Went to see him.
He had a house in Malibu on stilts over the ocean.

He collected rocks and books,
So rocks and books were everywhere you looked.
Now it reminds me of Picasso,
Who I heard also stashes everything,
And then moves out when the house gets too jammed.

My father's got five places now,
All jammed with goodies. His desk always has a candy
On it, somewhere, amidst keys, paper, typewriter,
Pocket-knife & fountain pen.
I guess he likes things.

Whereas my mother is into colors.
Perfumes.
Her imagination is entirely different
From his, so no wonder they were attracted.
Why they had to separate is another matter.

Maybe because they were both Virgos?
Since Virgos are supposed to have secret worlds ...

I don't know.
Both are artists.
Neither could care less that I write

Since they both do, too.
My mother remarried.
My father didn't—married to the typewriter though.
I think they both have fun.
My mother was seventeen, my father was thirty-six,

When they first married.
My father went immediately into the army.
My mother lived in New York.
I soon came into the world.
I remember being carried out onto the terrace at night

In my mother's arms.
At least I think I remember it.
How old was I?
Too little to know.
I remember my mother's mother was almost as young

As my mother.

MY FATHER WRITING

My father sits at his desk,
Or it is more like he is squatting there
When he is writing,
As if at any moment he might spring
From his position and up into the room.

He types quickly, in spurts—
Lights up a cigarette in between.
Coffee is always nearby.
He eats lunch on a card table
Spread with newspapers.

He reads while he eats,
Letting his mind rest for the next episode
Of his writing.
He cooks for himself and eats heartily,
Keeping himself strong for what is ahead.

In thirty some years, he has written fifty some books.
Not bad
For a man who never finished the eighth grade,
Never really knew his father,
And whose relatives, like himself, are all crazy.

MY MOTHER AND NEW YORK

My mother has New York in her blood
The way few women do.
Not the New York you or I know,
Something fantastic,
The greatest city in the world.

She grew up on the Upper East Side,
After spending her earliest years
With a foster parent, a Catholic woman named Genevieve,
In New Jersey.
She graduated from Dalton in New York

Having done a paper there on William Saroyan,
Whom she went on to marry the same year.
"I fell in love with your mother's past,"
My father once told me,
Having been an orphan himself.

My mother and my father must have made
A fine couple.
They went everywhere together.
The Stork Club sent me a silver spoon
When I was born.

That New York.
My mother lived it,
My father lived it,
The way only a few people could.
I heard about it later from my mother.

THERE ARE ANIMALS IN THIS AREA

There are animals in this area.
Other than you and me, I mean.
The other day I saw a deer.
And tonight I saw what looked like a big racoon,
Right outside our door.

FOR VOZNESENSKY

I dig you.
You've got a cosmic sense of humor.

What's purple and conquered the world?
Kubla Plum.

You and Yevtushenko are a couple of poet
Comedians, poet tragedians being

A little out of style.
Neither of you has even a mustache

To go by.
You do something to me.

The world seems to be reaching out
For the likes of poets, and you two

Are meeting its grip
In a warm and firm handshake.

We younger Americans hear you, too,
Though sometimes we don't admit it

Even to ourselves.
It's because we're a little too sophisticated,

But we aren't, really.
We are really just like you,

Only on the other side, America,
Living lives, having families.

Loving our wives, writing poetry.
Brushing our teeth.

Life is going by, as we go by
In it, living it, and digging you live it, too.

Poets are poets,
Not legislators, and such.

Fuck Government.
Poetry is alive, as we are—

The same head
On different bodies

Walking through our lives.
I salute you.

FULL MOON ODE

A full moon tonight.
And a poetry reading by two young poets
Who are really good, and Lewis and I and Bill
Suddenly feel old?
Probably not.

On Monday I'll be twenty-nine.
That's the age Shelley died at, I think.
And Stephen Crane.
You and I and Strawberry come home,
Find our house nestled in the dark with the lights on.

Time marches on,
Enough so that by this time,
I feel it's caught up with me,
And I know it as well as I know anything,
I guess.

If you push time around,
It pushes back.
It can kill you, too,
As I guess we all know
Since it's already killed a few of us.

My father is sixty-four this year.
My mother is forty-eight.
I'm writing long poems suddenly
For the first time in my life.
And we have a little girl who will soon be two.

She came home from the reading
Out of sorts.

We're, after all, just getting settled still,
And every outing tends to get to her more
Than it will in a little while.

MY GRANDMOTHER

My grandmother lives on Park Avenue now.
She's had a heck of a life.
She was brought up in a house on Gramercy Park,
But when she got knocked up with my mother
They kicked her out of the house.

She was sixteen, didn't know which way was up.
I don't know how she handled it, but she did.
A strong nervous system, I'd guess.
If I go up and see her now, she feeds me cottage cheese.
And honey.

English muffins. With real butter.
That's just coffee. If we come for dinner: chicken.
And she can make it better than anyone in the world.
No wonder she's put on some weight.
She's exactly my father's age.

And she loves him.
Sometimes I wonder how they would have done together
If he'd married her instead of my mother.
But he didn't, she didn't, and it couldn't have been.
You'd have to have a hole in your head to believe it could.

Now she wakes up in luxury, alone.
But that's probably part of the luxury.
People who are crowded when they're young
Probably need the room later,
Or so I imagine.

She keeps the place spotless.
Vacuums. And talks on the telephone.

She hates all her friends, but each one in a special way,
So you can tell she loves them.
Then she eats lunch.

At night she watches TV.
Sometimes she reads, but not often.
She has her relatives over a lot and they sit and reminisce.
They all look out of another era
Which they are.

When she gets to talking about the blacks,
You might as well fall asleep.
She's after them with a vehemence.
But what she's really mad at is life.
She had it too hard at first, it's too soft now.

FOR LEWIS MACADAMS

I can always count on you and Phoebe
To invite a few extra people
To any party we give. You two are the social couple
Here in Bolinas, as well as the mysterious,
Weird, insane, glamorous, captivating, delightful duo

You both just naturally are. And we count on you
To be. You're into politics, too.
And Phoebe knows poetry. A poem of hers on giving birth
Is in today's new issue of *The Paper.*
Last night you both were here for my birthday

And our housewarming combined. So were
A couple of other people I know only
Slightly. No matter. You know them perhaps slightly
Better than I do, and in that there is comfort.
The two of you are great at parties.

Phoebe threw a small toy at me at one point
Last night. I don't know why she did it, and I know
I won't ever know. She just did. You brought me
City Money, your first book, inscribed to me
with the words "Hell's Bells." I tell you,

I don't need to understand. The two of you
Are perfect, that's all. And if it's perfect mystery
Or perfect insanity, all the better.
We love you.
Keep that in mind, will you.

A NOTE

As a young boy I was skinny and shy, although my nature was already aggressive in some areas. I was a fair wrestler, solving a number of disputes by holding my opponent in a headlock which I would periodically tighten for half-a-minute or so, giving it all my might. My opponent would give up after a couple of these intervals, emerging pink-faced and, it seemed to me, mildly bewildered. Who, after all, could have anticipated this kind of hold from the likes of me. But perhaps that is only my imagination, perhaps every man imagines himself to be—or to appear to be—less than he actually is.

I was given IQ tests a number of times, and I did rather poorly. I remember a guidance counselor in junior high school looking askance at me, then back at my written profile, saying, "Well, you're a person of *some* intelligence." The weird thing was this old lady couldn't read anything aloud without stumbling and doubling back over her words again and again. I figured I was probably around as dumb as she was.

I remember one afternoon coming out of the school building on my way home and seeing a boy who seemed to me to look like me, except that his face was already dead from the life he had. He was standing before another, much larger boy, someone I thought of as good-natured and humorous, and he had his hand stuck in the top of his jacket. He said to the larger boy, in a thick New York accent: "You take one more step and I'll put a big nail in the middle of your head." The next thing I knew the boy was having his head banged against the sidewalk by the larger boy.

These are things I have never discussed with anyone, not even the several psychiatrists I went to in my early twenties. They are images and events that are central to my life, in that they will probably remain with me all my life, but I don't know what to do with them. I remember a girl I had hardly ever given a second look walking one day in full profile to the teacher's desk. There was a nearly audible gasp as a few of us beheld her full bosom. There was another girl, Gail Mazo was her name, who never said a word so far as I knew but one day was asked by the teacher to read her composition, which she did to everyone's total amazement. A natural writer.

FOR RICHARD BRAUTIGAN

Your writing reminds me
Of a beautiful garden,
Carefully tended.

On the side
Is the gardener, you,
Beaming proudly.

MY AUNT COSETTE

My Aunt Cosette is a saint.
She is a sweet woman of seventy-three,
A spinster with a sense of humor,
And a weakness for my father.

He bosses her around when he comes to stay
In his downstairs studio and bedroom
In the house he bought for his mother and her
When he made his first big money.

He's a difficult man
But she's known him all his life
And he never knew her
Before she was ten.

FOR GAILYN

You are the beginning and the end of
Every day for me. I see you all the time.
And in all that time
You have always looked as you look now,
No matter how much we've changed.

Your look is you.
It was probably there before you were born.
You arrived to fill it, to make it you.
And you have done it,
You are you.

I am me when I'm with you.
Even when we're in different places,
I know you're there.
Last night you and I got together again
For the first time in a while.

Today the sun is shining,
The trees are swaying green.
Life is the way it normally is
On earth. You are in the garden
Turning the soft earth.

Friendly Persuasion

FRIENDLY PERSUASION

The body and the mind
Have a talk together

And the mind convinces the body
To go out with it on a date.

Soon afterwards
The mind calls the body up on the telephone

And says,
"Why don't you drop by?"

"When?" the body asks.
"How 'bout this afternoon."

In no time at all the mind and the body
Are going steady.

Then they get married.
For a while they are very poor

And sometimes they have to go and stay at the body's folks'
        place
And then they have to stay at the mind's folks' place.

Neither one is a very good place to stay
They decide

And almost immediately they have a child.

MY FRIENDS

My friends, don't fear.
I love you
Like I love myself.
I love you like I love nobody else.

If you run into me downtown,
Know that like you,
I'm out for a good time.
Life is too short to waste on crying.

If my mood seems dour to you,
Remind me who you are,
Smile at me,
And my normal happiness will instantly return.

A man today has every right to be confused,
At least for an instant,
Just as he has a right to be brilliant—
After all, a man is a god in his own body.

A man is another toy of this universe,
But a man has friends—
People he likes to be with—
And they fill him with love to go on living.

ODE TO THE UNIVERSE

Let me know intimately
In my own way
A solitary passenger like any other
You've seen after me

And shown me another side of yourself already
Than I ever expected
Could it be you are me inside out
And Gailyn and Strawberry

No matter how or why or even what
You are larger than any night
More powerful than any god
I feel you advance and recede

In my own human weight
I know nothing now
But I'm learning to behave in your presence
To be aware of your life

ODE TO POWER

Power comes on strong
Pushes and pulls you anywhere it pleases
Before you realize what it is
Before you know what to do with it

A little later you are more familiar
Though it would be hard to say friendly
Fear is an old, old thing
Clarity is immobile

Power is everything, anything
It chooses to be
A flower, a man, an enemy or friend
It cuts through the universe effortlessly

And arrives at your side, at your feet
Be careful with it, treat it with respect
Yet be firm
Don't let it overpower you, use it

ROCK SONG

Leon Russell's got a lot of muscle
Cat Stevens sings it in.
John Lennon makes a melody
That lets the angels in.

Bob Dylan's got good karma.
Paul McCartney's putting it in.
Randy Newman's by the poolside
& Nilsson's swimming in.

Elton John sings a love song.
Leonard Cohen talks along.
Judy Collins is such a lady,
Stephen Stills such a man.

Neil Young's gettin' jumpy.
Donovan's under the sun.
Van Morrison's on the doorstep
In a whole new land.

ODE TO MICHAEL J. BRODEY

When you were writing checks to strangers
Taking the press and media on a holiday
Gailyn and I were down to nothing
Living with my grandmother on Park Avenue

"Write to him," she told me, "he'll probably send you
    something."
I affected cool, but a minute later was seated in a chair
    writing to you
On paper my grandmother brought me

A night or two later we watched you
Hanging out on the Johnny Carson Show
Delivering proclamations, very accelerated by what you had
    done
Everyone's mind was blown

I never sent that letter somehow
But my grandmother felt better that I had made the effort
We were able to get by a few more days there with your
    help
Now you're gone, apparently by your own hand

And I feel I've lost a distant friend
You gave money away, what an act
I tried to explain to my grandmother it was the best thing
    since Duchamp
Brought a shovel in off the street and sold it for art

PASTORALE

It takes nerve
To move into the suburbs;
Set up house,
Face the same faces

Day after day:
Especially without a car.
You need to abandon all reserve
And hitchhike downtown for

Your goods. People look on you
As younger, maybe, than you are,
Walking with wife and daughter
While everybody drives by.

But who knows. You get to know
The town, you keep fit, after all,
And the seasons pass without a hitch.
Your closest neighbor has five kids.

SOMETHING

My father collects rocks.
He keeps coins in quart jars,
Filled to the brim.
His sofa overflows with books.

Each day, it seems, he makes drawings.
Some are done like this: Hold the pen
Down and don't bring it off the page
Until the drawing is done, one

Continuous, circumnavigating, in-
Tersecting line. Time?
One of his favorite games is
"What time is it?"

I guess,
He guesses;
Then he checks his wristwatch.
Whoever's closest, wins.

I seldom do, but when it happens
He says, "You're in the groove."
He's been around a long time.
He must know something.

LOVE POEM

I wake up in the morning
I go to sleep at night
With you beside me

WHAT A SWEET THING

What a sweet thing a child is—
As sweet as new-mown grass.

TROUBADOUR

I sing my song solidly in time
I take the beat from the drummer
In my body and my mind
The line is a melody only I can find

The day rises boldly, my heart is good
The night comes swiftly, my love is true
I go my way singing for a nickel and a dime
The sun is a lyric, the moon is my sign

The planet echoes murder, the child gives all
The seasons have reasons, we sit and talk
The trees are blessings, the mountains are grace
The birds are a'twitter every single day

GAILYN'S BOUQUET

Gailyn picked a bouquet,
Just now,
Out on our Sunday walk.

Little white flowers
On long thin stems ...
Just like her, I thought.

NIGHT-TIME

My wife is reading, my daughter's asleep,
Spread like a little airplane across her bed.

The radio's on. The night outside is
Comforting, the end of another day.

JUDGE A MAN BY HIS ENEMIES

Judge a man by his enemies
Forget about his friends.
A man who's got a good enemy
Doesn't need a good friend.

His enemy stalks him
When he isn't looking,
So he learns to look
When his back seems turned.

His enemy will kill him
When he's on vacation,
So he learns to vacation
On his own hard work.

The next thing you know
His enemy is plotting
To do something crazy.
His enemy does it—

But it doesn't faze him.
He loves his enemy
The way he'd love a friend.
They're almost the same, in the end.

MADNESS

I used to believe that nobody was really crazy,
That people were all basically good. Sometimes it was
A question of coaxing them, a little, but in the end
You'd get back what you gave and more even.

But as I grew older I learned that's not always the case.
You have evil in this world as you have anything else.
I remember the first time I noticed someone was crazy.
It wasn't interesting, really; I only wanted to leave

And go some place else. There was nothing to discuss.
The fact is it was boring. I had no impulse to make myself
Clear because that wasn't possible—there was no inter-
Action at all; nothing but the rushing noise of a bird

Trying to escape a cage, its wing sticking out, or its head,
But never its whole self. The talk is self-obsessed.
Being inside the cage has made it a sudden stranger to the
        air,
And whatever appears in it. But the cage is not there

At all. There is only a person, one who looks deceptively
Like you or me, except for a certain deadness—
        recognizable
After a while—in the eyes. If you spend any time at all
You notice a tendency to repeat, the mind is trapped in a

Vicious circle, trying to make itself supreme over
Everything by accepting nothing but its own hysteria.
It would be sad, I suppose, except that it is uglier than that.
You find yourself looking away, after a while, and when you

Look again—you find the same thing. It goes on and on.
It has nothing to do with you. It has nothing to do with
      anybody,
Not even the person there in front of you. They are
      possessed,
Not by their own bodies, but by the evil that is very much

Part of this world. They are weak—or they were, I guess,
Before the evil entered them. Why else would they let it in?
But once it happens they acquire the power of what has
Entered them, the power of evil. I believe this power

Is no small consequence, as witness the evil of this world.
But I believe the power of good is of greater force, in the
      end.

I'M THE MISSISSIPPI

I'm the Mississippi. Nothing
Can stop me. Everything goes my way
Or I flow over, around, or under it,
Changing my dimensions as I go.

Trees, rocks, the animal and human kingdom
Are all passengers of my will. I treat them
As they treat me, loving the way I go on and on
Until I meet the sea. I'm the Mississippi.

Men sail me as I sail them, no better and
No worse. I'm a river, in the end, not a destination.
Nothing comes between me and my own motion.
I embrace it, and it becomes me, the Mississippi.

QUICK POEM

My daughter is alive
As I am alive
As my wife is alive

All of us
In the same time

SHAO'S BOOK

Shao's book holds the mind
To your heart, let's you see
Who you are reading, let's you
Be yourself reading him.

FOR BORIS PASTERNAK

Your spirit informs a new air, a new
Flavor. Russia couldn't fetter you; its
Difficulties became for you a crucible
In which you forged a new song

For the whole planet. You died
Suddenly famous after a lifetime known
Only to the few. I knew *Doctor Zhivago*
First as a movie, never guessing

What its pages held in store for me.
Your poetry I knew only as Russian—
And what can a Russian say to an
Armenian Jewish American? Only

That the leaves fall off the trees
Once a year; then, in spring,
They grow back on again, green.
Men & women walk around in

The sun and the rain. We all
Go to the grave one day. The earth
Is only one flavor of our eternity.
You have made it rarer to me.

OH TO BE IN LONDON

Oh to be in London
A city plain and true
With parks off nearly
Every avenue, with good

Places to eat among
The working people, a menu
To make a man feel good
And the noise of English

Everywhere in the air
In accents coarse &
Rare, and newspapers
That hold the world up

In better prose than
We're used to in America
That young nation that
Has nothing of London's

Understanding of all
Things, and the English
Character itself, a marvel
Of honesty in its way

SPRING SONG

In spring you get a feeling as if the body is deeply
Stretching itself, new cells coming into being overnight,
Thoughts of travel into the blue, dreams of old friends,
Faraway homes. It is a time of almost unbelievable

Joy, the sun outside shining, the night fragrant with
New bloom. No wonder men go a little crazy every year
Around this time. You need a strong sense of home to keep
You together, a loving woman to ease your entry into

This new season of your spirit. Sex reawakens out of
The half-sleep of winter; you find yourself making it
Again with a quickened sense of rhythm, greater tension
Between the magnetic fields of your bodies. And the little

One, your offspring, races around with a new seriousness
But then takes long, deep naps, letting you in on the fact
That this is a real transition for her, too, as she seems
To notice you differently, and love you, you notice, her
        father.

AS A CHILD I USED TO WANDER

As a child I used to wander
Among the rocks and boulders on the beach at Malibu
And today I walked and wandered through them up the
        coast
On the beach below the mesa in Bolinas
I smelled seaweed again

What a great smell it is
Sweet and pungent too
Strawberry probably is going to stop taking naps after a
        while
My mother has a genius for life
And she is an artist at it

I thought walking beside the ocean
One nostril inhaling "sea" the other "land"
The sun shining on the water
And then I walked up the cliff
Saw only one couple the whole length of the beach

My stepfather is Walter Matthau, a movie star
And a man with a gift for balance
He likes to gamble
Just as my father does and I do too
Though I don't go to the track I don't even play cards

A CHILD

A child
Is a mind
Apart.

PARABLE

I let my hair down
And then I took off my head.

LIFE IS NO ARRIVAL

Life is no arrival. The day goes,
Turning into night, reading—an arrival
Of a kind, I guess, if a book is good enough,
If it can fix life in its lines; as if life
Might ever offer the time for its own vision,

Revealed. But the action *is* an understanding,
Day in and day out, courting power, courting doubt.
The child works tirelessly each day learning the human
Vocabulary. She sleeps as we do, wakes fresh
For another bout with her angel and adversary.

Writing is only another thought too deep for
Thinking, moving into the moving lines before
It is known, before it is understood. Poetry
Surrenders to its flow, unknowing, innocent.
These lines are written on the run.

LIFE IS A DREAM

Life is a dream.
Boulders on the beach assume the form
Of animals. No man is certain. Death
Speaks in the wings, coaching, prompting

Emotion, the love of wood
Burning, the child's face waiting, laughing.
The sun comes up so many times, lighting
The life that is there to be seen.

We have been traveling through this tunnel
In eternity. Rocks persistently speak
To us, saying something so pure it is only
Feeling. This and that, this and that.

The buildings of the mind shut down
Before the advance of this truth.
We are here for good. There is no one
To be us instead. We are alive and dead.

FIST-FIGHT

You have a fist-fight
And you hit the other guy
Hard in the eye.
It starts to bleed.

Meanwhile, he's trying to
Scratch you or something.
He gets you under the neck
With his nails. You decide

To try a jab, but you're
Running out of
Stamina, acting like
Muhammad Ali

But backing away.
He can't hit you
But if the fight goes
Much longer you'll

Go to your grave.
You say to him,
"Hey, man, let's
Stop, okay?"

THE TOWN NEEDS A MAGAZINE

The town needs a magazine,
Russ and I agree one morning in Scowley's
Over breakfast. Then Russ, the shitkicker,
Starts getting philosophical; and I, being

The poet, start getting practical. Forget
Esthetics, I tell him, it's getting it out
That counts. He in turn looks at me gravely
As if I have not understood the deep

Community that makes this town tick.
We can use a mimeo machine in the Public
Utilities building; Patrick, the poet and
Barfighter, will run it off for us some night.

Susan, Russ's woman, will type it—on
Legal-size stencils, we decide—if Gailyn,
My wife, will look after Riviere, their
Little son, as well as Strawberry, our

Little daughter, the night we do it.
So we go out and collect the material:
I approach the poets, Russ the townsfolk—
And in a week we bring out a proud beauty.

THE LIVING DEAD

The living dead walk among us,
Speak our language, share the air
We breathe.

They enter our lives as if they were
Alive, and it is a moment or two
Before you recognize the chill
Of death's presence deep inside your body.

Time Pieces

GRINDING COFFEE

Grinding coffee was my favorite pastime
When I was three or four. I used to sit
On the kitchen floor with the coffee grinder
Between my knees, grinding and checking

My progress from time to time in the drawer
At the bottom where the ground coffee fell.
When I had finished and the drawer was full,
I smoothed it with my finger, contented.

AN IMMACULATE ROOM

I wake up in an immaculate room.
There is a chair against the wall
And an envelope on the seat.
The envelope is white; the rest

Of the room is grayish in the afternoon
Light. I have taken a nap, and I'm
Not quite familiar with where I am.
The envelope pricks my curiosity:

I keep wanting to go over and open it.
The room is so perfect, there is no
Noise. Finally I get up out of the bed
And walk over to the chair in my bare

Feet. I have gray pajamas on. I take
The envelope off the chair and open it,
Removing a small box, its only contents.
I open the box and it's filled with

Little envelopes. I take one of these out
And open it, but before I've finished
A razor blade slips out and cuts my palm.
I see the blood and scream for my mother.

DREAMS ON THE WALL

Dreams on the wall I saw
As a child and tried to explain
To my nurse, who told me
There was no such thing, the

Wall was white, not covered
With tiny cartoons I was seeing—
I see today as an adult, and wonder
What was wrong with that nurse.

MOVIES WHEN I WAS A KID

Movies when I was a kid
Weren't like movies are now.
I remember "Samson & Delilah";
It moved me with the deep

Goodness of the Bible. Delilah
Came through to me as a woman of unbelievable
Beauty, Samson as the most handsome man
I'd ever seen. Then there was

"Winchester '73." Here the hero was the rifle,
And western life in general. Chaps, spurs,
Horses and saddles. I could never follow
The plot of any of these movies, the textures

Were too involving. Now if I watch them
I see them entirely differently: Victor Mature
As Samson; Jimmy Stewart shooting from
Behind the rocks I saw first when I was a kid.

MR. STUMOLA

Mr. Stumola was my gym teacher when I was in the first
    grade
At Allen Stevenson School in Manhattan. I idolized the
    man,
And he seemed to take a fatherly interest in me. In gym
Class, once, we were all asked to assume our fighting
    stance.

I was somewhere in the back of a whole room of boys in
Lines. They wouldn't get to me for a long time so I could
Work on it, try to figure out the perfect, most impenetrable
Stance. By the time they got to me I had to be unwound, so

Tightly had I contorted myself against the enemy. Later,
In Van Courtland Park one afternoon, Mr. Stumola called
    me
Over and asked me who I wanted to fight of my classmates.
I wanted to pick one I thought I could beat but not one

Obviously weak. The boy I picked came over and we
    squared
Off—he hit me in the nose; it bled, and I rushed to the
Drinking fountain to clean it, my hand, my face. Mr.
    Stumola
Singled me out among the boys when we were all drilling a
    week later

On the school roof. "I want to shake hands now with a boy
Who got a bloody nose and didn't even cry." Then he said
My name. I was surprised—it seemed to have happened
So long ago in my child's-time that the gesture was almost
    empty.

SUMMER'S END

It was the end of a summer
We had spent at the house of friends.
We were saying goodbye, all us kids
In a line, waiting to shake hands

With an old, intensely irritable man.
I hadn't done very well with him
But I wanted to go out with sincere
Thanks, let him know I appreciated

His generosity to us all, that I was
In my own way not just a childish
Soul. I was ready, finally, to meet
This man and give him something

Of myself he hadn't suspected. Then
Just as my turn was coming up, my
Suit and tie all neat, my hair combed, I
Noticed I had hair tonic all over my hands.

There was no time to step out of line
And run and wash them. I was too close
To rub them on the grass, and I couldn't
Wipe them on the suit. I came up to

This man, so old he was seated in a
Chair, and we shook hands, my giving
Him all I could through my eyes. He
Made a noise, looked fiercely out at me,

And rubbed his hand on his pants.

MY FATHER OWNED A GUN ONCE

My father owned a gun once
And I saw it. I must have been six
And a half. It was a little automatic.
So small, I thought, to kill a man.

I wondered what he was doing with one.
Mom and he had got married again but there
Was tension in the house, a small mansion
In Beverly Hills. I taught myself to ride

No-handed on my bike, riding up and down
The bridle path that ran down the middle
Of North Rodeo Drive, where we lived.
It took one afternoon. My father

Had an office where he worked. It had
A large black leather sofa in it, which
He later transferred to his place in Malibu,
When they split up again and he bought it and

A house in Pacific Palisades for Mom, Lucy and me.

ERASERS

Erasers. The smell of them. The look
And smell of them. The girl with the big
Cylindrical one on her desk in front of me
Turns around and tells me, "You look just like

My boy friend." She looks just like her
Eraser. Chubby. And nice. Claudia. But how can
You get serious about a girl who comes on like that.
I fell for Betty, instead. Blond & colorful, tall.

She kept my heart beating like a hunter's
When I was seven. I wrestled someone in her
Defense—handsome opponent, luckily he
Couldn't wrestle. I was a serious kid.

MARTHA GOETZ

Martha Goetz was a friend of my mother's
Around the time of her second divorce from
My father: I was eight, and for a while we
Lived in a small apartment on Olympic Boulevard

In Beverly Hills. I went to a Catholic school, and played
In the alley with my friend Tommy (we found
A bullet once, wrapped it in a napkin, and took it
To the police station)—but all was not well, my self-

Image was slipping; I experienced occasional hyp-
Nogogic hallucinations (where all sound becomes
Demonized gibberish), and if Martha hadn't come along
And taken an interest in me, I might have struck out

On a life of loveless misdoing, understanding
Nothing. Martha, a woman with a daughter a little older
Than I, seemed to favor boys over girls, being
Only tolerant of Lucy (once accused her of

Cheating at Chinese Checkers). She was married then
To a man named Hayes, who had the perennial Beverly
Hills deep tan and seemed to favor very little indeed.
They had a painting over their dining room table, an early

Bernard Buffet I think, and Martha told me
A story about it. The painting was a grayish rendering
Of a plate, knife, fork & spoon, set on a table. Martha
Told me the reason the color was so gray was that the artist

Was down to his last tubes of paint and had no money
When he painted it, hoping to make a sale. She became

A benefactress, by implication, and she truly was, most
    likely
Is still. She took me to baseball games—the

Hollywood Stars versus the Los Angeles—what? It slips
My memory. They were a local minor league of that time.
More importantly, she patiently taught me how to keep
A box score, so that while I flunked the third grade

At the Catholic school, I didn't lose the sense that I could
Learn. I was deeply satisfied to be able to do something
Correctly, and she seemed to take pride in me as well.
My mother was going through her own hell at the time

And was unable to give Lucy or me much of herself.

WHEN I WAS EIGHT IN BEVERLY HILLS

I stole a machine gun water-pistol out of the drugstore
Where my mother went to the hairdresser's upstairs
And I read movie magazines up there waiting for her. They
    were great...
Debbie & Eddie, Bob & Natalie ... I came back one
    afternoon

Without my mother, and kneeled down to look at this
    thing: a machine gun
Water-pistol. It was the biggest water-pistol I'd ever seen. It
    was on a rack
Below the counter with other toys, and I noticed nobody
    was tending
The counter it was below—so if I walked sideways
    out... the door

Was right there. After about half-an-hour (I practically went
    to sleep
With quandariness), I did it. I walked sideways out of the
    drugstore
With the machine gun water-pistol in front of me, and ran
With it home. Then I didn't know what to do with it. I
    buried it, quickly.

MARLON BRANDO

My mother knew Marlon Brando
And one day he came to take her
And me and Lucy all to the beach.
My mother wanted me to wash my face

Before we left, but he said no, why
Don't you let him just go, he looks
Okay; and I thought, Jesus, this guy
Is just like they say he is

In the movie magazines.

MY NEIGHBORHOOD:
PACIFIC PALISADES IN THE FIFTIES

Jay Danley would lie around all day on his folks' lawn.
Fran Loetterle and I would complain to each other about
  him.
Chris and Martin Andrews were English brothers up the
  hill.
Mike Mandell had a slow way about him. I once heard his
  father,

The psychiatrist, tell someone that a black widow spider
Climbed up your leg and bit you on the penis. I'm still
  looking out
For one. There was a strange blond woman whose car
  rolled
Down the hill one morning, with no one in it—

And crashed into a garage. Then one night she drove it
Into the Loetterles' garage door. She had a little son
Who once unleashed a stream of obscenity,
Surprising everyone. He was rumored to be a pyro-

Maniac. Our next door neighbors, the Gumps, were a quiet
Model couple with two young daughters. My mother's
  room
Looked onto their bedroom, and she was heartened one
  morning
To hear Mickey, then see her, the perfect homemaker, stark
  naked,

Screaming at George, Kathy & Gail: "Oh, fuck you! Fuck
  all of you!"

I PLAYED LITTLE LEAGUE

I played Little League.
I was an outfielder, but once
They brought me in to pitch.
I astonished everyone by throwing the ball so slowly

No one could
Hit it. At the plate, I was only
Average. But once, when my father came
And sat watching, I hit a home run.

ONE NIGHT

One night when I was nine or ten
I woke up because someone was playing
The piano in the living room. I must have
Lain there in my bed listening for, oh,

A half hour or more, wondering from time
To time just when it was going to end and
Meanwhile trying to decipher a melody
In the music I was hearing. It just went

On and on, and finally, though I was trying
To control it, trying to outlast this marathon
Interruption of my sleep, I began to get mad
And want to go out and stop whoever was playing

With some strong words. I got up out of my bed,
Opened my door without making a sound, and tiptoed out
To have a look at the source of this insanity. I knew
The piano would face me, so whoever was sitting there

Wouldn't see. I looked into the room, and there was
Some man playing with my mother sitting next to him.
As angry as I was, it was somehow touching; the man
Had his jacket off and was trying to play the music

With apparent difficulty. It just didn't sound like
Anything in particular, though I knew it was
Classical. I stood there in my pajamas, watching
This scene for some time, unable to say anything,

And then I turned around, and returned to my room,
And got back into bed, and listened and listened,

Wondering who is this guy, anyway, and why is he doing
    this.
The next day my mother told me it was Jim Agee

And he was playing Mozart.

THE SUMMER I WAS TEN

Kay Kendall was my mother's best friend
I was in love with her.
She gave me a platinum ring too big for any of my fingers.
"He'll lose it," my mother said.

We were staying with my aunt in Switzerland.
Her son Hubert hit Lucy in the forehead with a rake. She
    screamed
And ran into the house.
I put the ring under my pillow and it disappeared.

I wandered all around where my aunt lived,
Looking for the ring. I opened the door to my mother's
    room
And saw Kay sitting naked. She covered her tits.
I kept crying about losing the ring.

I went to visit the Chaplins. Lucy stayed with Mom.
I picked up Josephine and she wiggled out of my arms
And dropped onto the ground. Screaming, she ran
Into the house. A little later, Chaplin came out

And took me aside. We went for a walk together.
"You must tell me everything that happened
Because she may die," he said. I told him, feeling
I would never be able to get over killing someone.

At the edge of the estate Michael and I threw rocks
Through a wire fence at a beautiful girl. One
I threw hit her and she ran into the house,
Covering her face. Had I blinded someone?

The doctor said Josephine was all right. I left,
And Mom and Kay and Lucy and I all took a train
To Portofino with money Mom had made
Acting in Paris while I was at the Chaplins'.

On the train Kay told me she had no sense of smell
Or taste. How could she live this way, I thought.
She was colorblind too. I wished I could
Disappear into her and give her my senses.

In Portofino I hit Lucy. She started crying.
I told her to stop or I would hit her again.
She kept crying so I hit her again.
She started crying louder. My mother came in.

There was a man who sold jewelry on the piazza.
His eyes were so blue it was hard to look at them.
I saw a girl walking in a black jersey with her nipples
      bouncing.
Lucy told me to stop walking for a minute; then it was all
      right.

That night she had appendicitis.

THIRTEEN

I was thirteen, filled with an impossible will
To achieve. Not in school. There I was barely
Alive—a saint, an idiot. But in photography
Which struck me early as something beautiful to do.

I woke at five one morning to carry out the task
Of photographing snow before taking the bus to school.
I bundled up in the dark, my body thrilled to be alive
With intention while the rest of the family slept.

I hit the street at exactly dawn, the light on
In the corner candy store. There an old fat couple shuffled
To organize the morning deliveries. I bolted across
The empty street, walked a few blocks

And arrived. At the 96th Street entrance to Central Park.
Fifth Avenue a gray shroud behind me, I plunged
My boots into the two feet of undisturbed snow.
I wanted to photograph the real thing.

Dogs appeared: two German Shepherds cavorting
In the white expanse, trees the eye's only relief.
It was as if I had come out to photograph blindness.
I shot two rolls, slowly. And I went to school.

THE FIRST TIME I TRIED TO HAVE SEX

The first time I tried to have sex
I had a problem. I took it
As confirmation of everything else I knew about myself
Up to then. I was empty.

I walked to the bus stop in the rain
Remembering a photograph of Elizabeth Taylor reclining
in Montgomery Clift's lap. I imagined I
Was Montgomery Clift.

From then on I became conscious
Of my penis in a way I'd never been before.
I noticed every minute stirring, every
Grade of erection

For about a year. Then I gave it up. Soon
I was getting turned on again, hardly
Noticing it. It was as if I'd been trying
To learn how to breathe, interrupting

The natural flow of breath.

AS FOR FIGHTS

As for fights, I've had only a few.
The first time Bert McManus hit me
In boarding school, I saw stars—
A beautiful cluster breaking in my head.
The second time he hit me I saw them again.

Bert had a good one-two. I retired at fifteen
Like a permanent wrestler when boxing came in—
Hitting someone in the face seemed an awful thing.
Then one night at a party when I was nineteen
Bill Janeway let me get a good one in.

He sat down in a chair behind him, called me immature.
I knew I felt better.
Then there was one with my stepfather Walter,
An old street fighter who could have slaughtered me
That night on upper Broadway, but lucky for me that
        wasn't his thing.

The last time, at a party drunk, I hit a guy who turned out
        to be
An Olympic wrestler. Another guy hit me. I laughed
Because he had no punch, and I didn't know him.
A little later, I fell down a flight of stairs.
Since then—nothing, though I think of it every so often.

MY FIRST ACID TRIP

My first acid trip happened one summer night
in Woodstock, New York in 1965. Four of us
Took it—Chris and Kim, Karen and me.
I started dancing to do something while

Waiting for it to come on. The first thing
That happened was that Karen told me she
Wanted to talk with me, alone. We went into
The little room with the big desk where we'd

Lived together most of the summer, and Karen
Sat down on the bed and looked at me. The light
Was on and her face was very vivid, the color
Of her skin very white and pink where the

Color rose up. I could suddenly see what Modigliani
Had been painting, the image plus his own nervous
System acting on it. Van Gogh and Soutine. She
Said, "Strange things are happening," and told

Me she could see tractor marks going down the side
Of my face. She was seventeen, I was twenty-one.
All I cold see was this vividness, and then
I looked into her eyes and what she was seeing took

In me. Her face began to contort and ugliness
Spill from it violently—I looked away. I knew I
Couldn't go through twelve hours of this. I looked back
And told her what I had seen, and that I would

Get up and have Chris come in. The rest of the
Trip we avoided each other and, really, it marked

The end of our being together, though we stayed with
Each other longer. I went out and saw Kim, a blond

Girl, sitting on the living room sofa all wrapped up
In a fur of some kind. She looked like an animal,
Purring. Chris came in again, then Karen, and the four
Of us stood in various shifting postures like panels in a

Comic strip: He looks at her, and she looks at me.
I look at him, and she looks at her looking at us.
Every instant changing, each as famous as we all were
To each other. Then I put my hands over my eyes and told

Everybody I was going back to the beginning,
When I first started. I see myself racing through
History, back and back, while the colors flashed
At the side of my vision—and then there was

A brilliant, kaleidoscopic explosion: It was a pinball
Machine that's been beaten and lights up and flashes.
A little later, I went back
Into the little room and sat at the desk,

Put a piece of paper in the typewriter and started
Typing. I was having a wonderful time: the words
Were different than they'd ever been, textures
That scrambled and unscrambled in my brain.

I gotta do some more, I said out loud and wrote.
But it's not morning yet, I heard Karen say and wrote.
But I gotta do some more/Whether it's snoring more
Or morning yet, I finished in my head and typed out.

I was ecstatic. I felt physically better than I
Had ever felt in my life, better than I had ever
Dreamed of feeling. My life was going to work out,
No matter what happened.

THREE PSYCHIATRISTS

I went to three psychiatrists.
The first, a black man, got me out of the draft.
The second, author of a book called *Psycho-*
Analysis and the Artist, told he he would make me

A business success. I replied that I was interested
In poetry. So was he, he told me, when he was young
Like me. Later his reasoning became clearer to me.
When you charge $35 for each session, you have an
    obligation

To make your patient successful. Otherwise he
Can't continue. The third and final one, Robert
Thorne, did a lot for me, and I came to understand his
    work
As a kind of art form. He knew what he was doing.

Leading me, by doing so little, to the day I could no longer
Remember what I wanted to say—he had become my
Demon, in front of me. When I confronted him directly,
Speaking to him, he gradually came out from behind my

Fantasy. Another person. This is the moment I remember
When I think of analysis. If I had gotten to know him
Before projecting my fantasy on to him, I could never
Have experienced my own obsessions in his person—

So he remained relatively quiet all that time, waiting.

MARBLEHEAD

The first time I walked into the bookstore
I bought a book. The man I bought it from,
Who looked to be around my own age,
Said it was a good book. At the time, the shop

Had just opened; there was a smell of wood
And shellac still in the air from making the shelves.
The man was small with jet black hair and very white skin
Where he didn't shave. We had just moved into town

From New York. Gailyn was pregnant with Strawberry.
For a while we lived in a guest house (one night
We heard a couple making it in the next room) and then
We moved into the upstairs apartment in a widow's house.

The fellow who ran the bookstore's name was Frank.
He called the place Parnassus and posted poems on the
        window
From time to time. I went in now and then, and then
Stopped altogether. It was as if the store were part of his

Insides, I felt, walking inside it. The town was Marblehead,
Massachusetts. We stayed less than a year. Gailyn got her
Labor pains too early one morning to call a taxi, so the
        police
Drove us through the deserted streets at top speed to the
        hospital.

CAMBRIDGE 1971

We came back to Cambridge with a little baby,
And $500 my stepfather gave me. We needed
To find a place to live in before we went
Broke. We checked into a hotel even though

We had an offer of a place to stay the night
From a girl we met in the Corners of the Mouth,
Where we ate a macrobiotic dinner. I knew the pressure
Of a hotel bill would make me move to find an apartment

Quickly. I got up the next morning, left Gailyn
And Strawberry in the room to go out and get
A paper. I didn't know the new *Phoenix*
Was just out when I bought a copy from a

Local street hawker. I scanned the apartments
And found three possibilities, among them the one
We saw and took immediately that evening.
It was a little three-room place with good light

In it. It was spring, and we moved in happy
To be back in the city we'd lived in first
Together. We were exhausted from having a
Child and for a year we mainly rested there,

Taking a daily trip into Harvard Square.

YESTERDAY

Yesterday we went into Sausalito to have lunch with
Gerard & Marcy, and do some shopping. I went into The
    Tides
To look at the books the minute we got off the bus; I
    bought
Rolling Stone, and looked through the new biography of
    Kerouac

By Ann Charters, looked in the index and found my name
    listed
With two page numbers beside it, both in connection with
the *Paris Review* interview. Then I went upstairs to see
The poetry, and bought Rod Taylor's book that got the rave

in *Poetry* by Thom Gunn. Then we walked about a mile
Up Bridgeway to Olive, where Gerard & Marcy live at
The top of number 516, only a little way up the hill.
Gerard greeted us at the door, the picture of health

Through poetry; Marcy turned out to be tall with big
Knockers, and sweet and interesting, too. We started
Out talking about the *Time* cover story on Carlos
Castaneda which Gerard refused to read, and Marcy

Just scanned—she immediately gave us the magazine
To take home with us. Gerard had corrected the cover
To read "Magic is Reality" instead of "Magic and Reality."
I said something about how, all objections aside, the cover
    of *Time*

Was *power.* Gerard said he thought it wasn't a good
Use of power. He showed us a new book called

Wheels of Light he had had printed in India while he was
    there,
And just gotten a copy of after the long wait of shipment by
    boat.

Then Marcy brought in a beautiful platter with egg salad
And tuna salad, avocado slices on the side. Rye bread.
Tea with honey. A fabulous feast. After luxuriating
Awhile in the afterglow of our satisfied appetites, Gailyn

And I decided we should go down the block and look at the
    stores
While Gerard and Marcy prepared to leave for Gerard's
    reading
That night in Santa Cruz. I decided to take the gallon can
    for
Kerosene while Gailyn with Strawberry looked in the yarn
    shop. It was

Raining, a little, as it continued to do on and off
All day. I had to walk farther to a gas station than I
    thought,
And the first one didn't have any. We use it in our lamps,
And the gas station in Bolinas has been out of it for a week

And doesn't know when it'll get any more. The second
Place had some, filled up the can, I paid the 88¢ and
Walked back to the yarn shop, passed it in fact, turned
Around and walked up the steps and in out of the rain.

I had a little dirt on my face and Gailyn told me where
To wipe it off. We put her shopping in a plastic bag kindly
Offered by the young woman proprietor and when I asked
    what
Time it was she offered to call, then remembered she

Had a clock in back and went back there, and came
And told us it was ten after two, leaving just enough time
To get a little shopping done in the health food store down
The street (hiziki, shampoo) before going back to get a

Ride into Sausalito proper with Gerard and Marcy on their
Way to Santa Cruz (first they'll pick up Andrei, Alice
And little Lucian Codrescu in San Francisco, who have
Decided to go along for the reading). This time Marcy

Opens the door, after glimpsing us through the big living
        room
Window on our way up. Gerard and I sit in back with
The straw bag of ours filled with shopping, kerosene tank,
Strawberry's bottle and food Gailyn's bought for her.

We pull out of the driveway and Gerard tells us how, on
        Monday,
He's going to have to go under at the dentist's for some
Expensive bridgework. Marcy is a good driver, I think,
And Sausalito comes along quickly and we have our fond

Farewells and get out of the yellow BMW, telling them
To come up and have a meal with us in Bolinas, and
Thank you. And then we go shopping. I spend
A long time in The Tides again and really get bored

Before Gailyn comes back with Strawberry with new
Shoes she's bought her. I start holding Strawberry and she
And I go into a restaurant while Gailyn goes to look
At another store. I order a french hamburger and a small
        coke.

And when it arrives I take it in one hand, Strawberry in the
        other arm,

And sit down in the one place available, opposite a man
	who looks
About my age. We nod at each other and while I bite into
	the
Hamburger (getting ketchup at the ketchup counter is
	going to be

Too difficult, I decide) he asks Strawberry what her name
	is.
I tell her to tell him, but she just sits looking beautiful, and
	finally
I tell him her name and he says, "Is that right, that's a nice
	name."
"Thank you," I say. Later he offers her one of his french
	fries,

First clearing it with me that it's all right, and I realize I
Should have gotten her an order in the first place. Then
Gailyn comes in, somewhat startling the guy with her blond
Beauty I think, and settles in a chair diagonally opposite me
	at

The next table. The good fellow immediately offers to
	switch
With her, and they do. She orders french fries for
	Strawberry
And hot cocoa which she and I split, realizing I am going to
	yang out,
Speaking macrobiotically, on all the meat and eggs I've
	been eating

Unless I temper it with some sweets. Then we go to a store
Almost next door to buy some sandals for Gailyn, really
	nice ones.
She's found a good natural sponge for $4.50 while
	Strawberry

And I were in the restaurant. We've left our straw bag all

This time in back of the counter at The Tides, and we
    decide
To leave it a little longer—Gailyn goes in to make sure it's
    still
There, it is—until we get the bus back in a little while.
Meanwhile, we walk up the street, and go into The Crepe
    Place.

I order a banana, Gailyn orders a strawberry. And it turns
Out they are both sort of ice cream sundae crepes, if you
Get the picture. They're pretty good though, and I can
Feel the sugar interacting with the salt inside me, and I
    figure

If I don't die, I'm going to be just right. Then we walk on
To an embroidery-needlework shop where Gailyn looks
    around
And I sit down with Strawberry. A large woman comes
Over and says, "I assume you are … waiting?"

Yes, I tell her, and she interacts briefly with Strawberry.
It seems that she is trying to impress everyone with her
Heavy vibe but she just seems pompous, and
I pick up a leaflet telling how the government is trying

To outlaw vitamins (to save the commercial food industry?)
And ponder. The old woman probably was truly great,
    getting
This nice store started when there were only a few people
Interested. Then I hear her greet someone with the words

"Good evening" and wonder what time it is, since our
Bus leaves at 5:33. I get up holding Strawberry
And ask one of the younger women if she knows the time.

She goes and looks behind the window and tells me almost

5:25. Gailyn rushes to make her purchase, and we quickly
Walk back to The Tides. I hand Gailyn Strawberry, she
Crosses the street to the bus stop—and I go in, get
Our straw bag, and come out and cross the street to join
    her

In the little bus stop shelter, where there are three bruised
And battered alcoholics, one standing holding forth. They
Are all around my age, and the one standing seems to have
Said something to Gailyn regarding getting himself to
    Bolinas

And now looks to me for corroboration fingering the map
    on
The wall. I look at him with no interest and say
Yeah. I see the bus coming, tell Gailyn, and when its door
Opens, the drunk jumps on and we follow him, my getting

The two transfers necessary for the Bolinas bus at
Marin City, the next stop. The drunk is at the very back.
Gailyn has herself and Strawberry on one side where
There are an empty two seats parallel. I sit down

With the straw bag, and in a few minutes the
Driver calls out "Marin City" and we make our way off
And into another little shelter, which Gailyn remarks is a
Pretty nice cabin. The drunk has forgotten to get off

The bus, if he is going to Bolinas, but I don't want
To give him any assistance. He rides off stretched out
In back, looking straight ahead. The big dummy needs
A few indications, right? Gailyn agrees, and I see a bus

Down a ways, go out and signal to it, wondering what

102

It's stopping for down so far, and whether it's going to stop
At the shelter. I run down a ways and it drives
Up toward me and I see it says Bolinas, down in the corner

Of the window, the little hand-painted sign the bus always
      has
For some reason, and I signal it and the driver
Signals me up ahead, so I run back to the shelter
And we get on, I hand him the transfers. He immediately

Starts talking about the little babies—Strawberry's asleep
In Gailyn's arms; she takes the first window seat,
I take the one on the other side—that come on asleep, and
      miss
His reckless driving. I say, "Well, take it easy tonight,
      because

We want her to get home safely," smiling at him, and he
      goes
On talking to the old lady sitting on the side seat almost
Opposite him, who laughs amiably at my remark. The bus
Ride home is nice, getting darker and darker as we go

So that by the time we get in it's dark. We get off,
Thanking the driver who offers us some candy we refuse
And immediately get a ride up the mesa right to
Laurel Road. I get the mail out of our box,

We go in the back door of our house, glad to
Be back in the quiet, sweet smelling country.
Gailyn puts Strawberry in her bed in her room
And we unpack slowly, fill our kerosene lamps,

Talk about everything. I make a fire in the little
Two burner stove next to the gas stove, and then I
Take a shower. When I come out Gailyn's settled

In the living room reading the Laura Ingalls Wilder book
She found at The Tides. I decide I should work on
My novel—a little every day—and I do that

First at the kitchen table next to the fire, then moving
Into the living room. When I finish I show Gailyn
The new chapter, she likes it, and we begin to
Move into the bedroom. I set a kerosene lamp on the

Little table on wheels (Strawberry's toy) right next to
My side of the bed, undress, and get in—still wearing
A tee shirt and socks—and huddle for a minute to
Get warm. Then I start reading the Castaneda story

In *Time* while Gailyn goes to sleep. He has told them
Lies about his life, which they discover and confront
Him with and he in turn justifies by saying that
Truth is not a matter of facts. The article is

Somehow mind-opening in the way the books are,
And I wonder for a while about what I'm doing,
After blowing out the lamp and setting it on the bureau,
Returning the table on wheels to its place in the living room

And getting back into bed to go to sleep. Castaneda
Is right, the truth is subjective. But I guess I've
Chosen to make mine correspond to the known facts
Of the matter, since that's what comes through to me.

O My Generation

CREAM'S SONG

Little baby, lying peaceful, in her Daddy's folded arms,
As he moves from room to room, thinking on and on and
    on;
Little baby, lying quiet, with her eyes shut almost tight;
It's her Daddy doing the thinking—she seems to feel all
    right.

Little baby, fast asleep now, as her Daddy keeps going
    round,
Moving from room to room to kitchen, where her Mama's
    cooking food.
Her big sister's on the table, watching Mama real close;
The household's all in order—it's just Daddy that's like a
    ghost.

Little baby, keep on sleeping, there's no need to fret or stir;
Your Daddy's just feeling funny inside this big old world.
There's no need to be uneasy or even on your guard;
The world's got its own motion—it'll take you for quite a
    ride.

POEM

I have lived to read Pasternak,
to practice sobriety as a pleasure,
to drink deeply of the well of human time,
with its children and other secrets.

The world is revealed to me daily,
in a meticulous profusion, excluding
nothing, no one. All is infinitely large
and small, the center ungraspable,

electric, at either extreme. My mind
contains the notes and figures of someone
I know I am, while I go on
somehow another, and another,

I can't keep up, but do keep going,
doing whatever must be done for myself,
my wife, the children we share as
miracles of our time together.

POEM

To walk with death,
Hand in hand,
Like a child
And its Raggedy Ann.

SAWING THE WOOD

To Russ & Susan

Sawing the wood
So I could be doing something
While just being alive

Sawing the wood
I feel a bird brush by
On the air above my hair

Sawing the wood
So I can think without
Going crazy

Sawing the wood
Because it's good
For my soul

Sawing the wood
Because I'm an ordinary man
In an ordinary world

Sawing the wood
Because my body and my mind
Are one

Sawing the wood
So my blood can move
So my blood can move

Sawing the wood
So I can understand
The nature of time

Sawing the wood
Because unsawed
It won't fit the stove

Sawing the wood
So I can remember
Everybody

Sawing the wood
In order to be
A big success

Sawing the wood
So I will have something
To teach my children

Sawing the wood
So I can be
Completely myself

Sawing the wood
Because I am thirty
Years old

Sawing the wood
To make politics
Ridiculous

Sawing the wood
To make me
Resilient

Sawing the wood
Because two is better
Than one

Sawing the wood
Because the gas
Is almost gone

Sawing the wood
Because life is but a dream
And I am alive

Sawing the wood
Because I'd rather be thin
Than famous

Sawing the wood
Because it is the only good cause
I know

Sawing the wood
Because it keeps my demons
At bay

Sawing the wood
To keep contact
With the saw

Sawing the wood
To know what the fire
Comes from

Sawing the wood
Because it is as good
As music

Sawing the wood
Because I aspire
I aspire

Sawing the wood
Sawing the wood
Sawing the wood

Sawing the wood
Because something tells me
To do it

Sawing the wood
To be alone
With everything

Sawing the wood
To feel the sun
On things

Sawing the wood
Because life is short
And life is long

Sawing the wood
To see the forget-me-nots
When I raise my head

Sawing the wood
To make good
Even better

Sawing the wood
To give the beat
A meaning

Sawing the wood
Because in an hour
It will be dark

Sawing the wood
Because my daughter comes out
To talk to me

Sawing the wood
Because nothing
Is so fulfilling

Sawing the wood
To get behind
The headlines

Sawing the wood
To be a little tired
After a while

Sawing the wood
To grow old
And wise

Sawing the wood
To make one thing
Into another

Sawing the wood
To get to the bottom
Of the pile

Sawing the wood
Because once I was a boy
And now I am a man

Sawing the wood
Because my father
Is older than me

Sawing the wood
Because my mother
Is older than me

Sawing the wood
Because my wife
Is inside sewing

THE NIGHT

The night is so
empty, and bright,
filled with thin air
and tiny stars deep
in the distance
that is infinite,
that has no end
like no mind, and yet
here I am, within it,
here, breathing, alive
and thoughtless
as the stars themselves.

FRIENDSHIP

Friendship makes its aims
The opposite of claims;
It seeks not to hold
But to unfold all that time

Keeps stored in its name;
To allow each his moment
In the sun, knowing the warmth
Will reflect on all who stand by.

No friend will call down another
From the perils or raptures of his climb;
It is not a friend's place to measure
But only to divine his own nature

In all his friends' designs. He sees
To believe, and not to question
Or uphold—to stitch the world fast
With affection.

WE ARE HUNGRY

to President Ford

I

We are hungry for Shakespeare.
We are hungry for clouds passing in the sky.
We are hungry for a cup of coffee, a sandwich, and a smile.
We are hungry for more and more radio while we drive.
We are hungry for a home, safe and secure.

We are hungry for a nice cold glass of milk.
Milk has something for every body.
We are hungry for more movie stars.
Marlon Brando can't be expected to do everything.
We are hungry for flashlights and pocket combs.

We are hungry for teachers.
And we are even hungrier for students.
After all, what would a teacher do without a student?
We are hungry for clothespins, hammers, and lipsticks.
No, not lipsticks, and no more bras.

We are also tired of underwear.
It makes no sense to hem the body in needlessly.
We are hungry for a new pair of shoes.
Or perhaps hiking boots this time around.
We are hungry for small fires.

And a campsite full of warm humanity.
Dogs, crickets, birds in the morning, etc.
We are hungry for dried vegetables you make into soup.
A tree looks beautiful.

We are hungry for well-behaved children.

We are hungry for newer art forms that introduce men and
        women
To each other for the first time as equals.
We would like to get to know the medical profession a lot
        better.
Is there a doctor in the White House?

We are hungry for good marriages.
But perhaps divorce is a healthy solution in certain cases.
After all, why prolong needless suffering?
We are hungry for brooms, flowers, and candles.
The color yellow makes us happy.

We are hungry for devices that keep the baby happy.
Or does every baby only wish to be wrapped up tight?
We are hungry for toys and candy.
Balloons, pennies, nickels, dimes, loose change of all
        varieties.
Paper money is also good.

We are hungry for warm drugstores.
And interesting personalities.
Not just television.
But we are hungry for television too.
We are hungry for red, white, and blue.

We are hungry for spiritual enlightenment.
Wood and rock are important parts of our world.
Paper and pencils, typewriters and carbon paper are fun.
A hatchet is useful in chopping wood.
We are hungry for sweaters.

II

Neighbors cannot lie to each other if the town is to survive.
And our country is only a neighborhood in this universe.
The stars answer us every night.
Either in the sky or on the nightly line-up.
We are a civilized country at heart.

No one wishes to be made a fool of by his neighbor.
Good fences may or may not be important
But Robert Frost was right about one thing—
There are miles to go before we sleep,
Miles to go before we sleep.

After all, we are alive.
Our days are filled with ups and downs,
Reversals and run-arounds,
Midnight telephone calls and midnight diapers.
Our lives are rich and various.

A true friend is the finest thing in the world.
And we make new friends all the time.
The Golden Rule always works
Though sometimes it demands patience.
We know ourselves inside out.

We believe in money, and yet it is only love.
What else would it be—for everybody to want it so much?
And we have made a rule to always reward those who try
        hard enough.
Our land sings with character.
It dances with a natural rhythm.

We are only the latest in a long line
From the President on down.
And we talk to the dead as well as to the living.

We number ourselves among the lost and the found.
We are happy and unhappy.

The moon is our finest sermon.
And it informs us of our mortal cycle.
We are ready to die and to be reborn
Every day.
You can't always get what you want.

But you usually get what you need.
The universe seems to carry a pocket snapshot of each of
    us
And know all our names by heart.
We accept evil because we accept good.
We can't hold a grudge for more than five minutes.

Our power is our delight in each other,
Our children, our artists, and our politicians.
We are never taken in by anything phony.
But we are not above loving our phonies
Along with everybody else.

The prisoners laugh at the same shows
As the more successful criminals.
We all have the same things at heart
Though we are worlds apart.
The Indians are our real ancestors.

III

Earth, air, fire and water are what we are made of.
That, and whatever else comes along.
We all like doing things well.
The best things in life are free.
Going to sleep, for instance.

Or waking up.
Making love with a partner we understand.
Having the mortgage payment on time.
Having the house in order.
Breathing deeply.

Everything costs money.
But money is only work.
And we are always working.
If we are underpaid,
We have found ways of getting around it.

Welfare, for instance, is a wonderful temporary solution
Even if it lasts all our lives.
We love music and bright colors.
No one denies us money
For being ill-tempered.

We love our naked bodies.
And the flowers and food in our gardens.
We like to dress with a characteristic flourish.
And comb our hair in ways that suit us.
Our world is busy with work.

Yet we remain hungry.
We are hungry for sorrow-in-joy
As well as joy-in-sorrow.
Everything seems to please us.
The old world of our fathers is a delight.

The new world of our prophets is amazing.
We await greetings from outer space
And we receive them, from time to time.
Infinity is beyond thought
But we love it anyway.

The seasons have brought us our knowledge of time.
Time is a god in our lives.
Our pleasures have informed us of the nature of space.
And now it seems there is no difference
Between space and time.

We are hungry for transition
As in Shakespeare's time.
Because we are here to learn.
Experience is the best teacher, it is said,
And the universe is always right up to date.

We are hungry for all you can share with us.
The world is only our backyard.
We are hungry for your prayers for us
As we pray for you.
We are hungry for everything.

POEM

I don't want to be a seer
And fly through the universe
I just want to be a man
And stay here
And let my time be open
To your time as yours is
Open to mine
And the children grow up
Inside our lives
And the house goes through
Its karma
And friends and neighbors
Successes and failures
Birds and learning
All intertwine within
The daylight and the nighttime
And I look out to see
The same tree
Differently each time

CHAPLIN'S SMILE

Chaplin's smile at the end
Of *City Lights*

Love and tragedy
Learning and yearning

The rose between his teeth
His bitten beliefs

The pale film of his intensity
His own strong corner

Of the immensity of life
And of death

In the city lights
We had dreamed

WALKING DOWN MARKET STREET

You see
A face like a moon
A face like a spoon
A face like a tree
A face like a storm
A face like a cloud
A face like mother
A face like—
      faces like everything
You have ever seen
The swarming mass of humanity
So naked in their various clothing
The world of the city before them
And you, you too
With the pavement beneath your feet
With your intentions
Your good and bad
Everything you've learned to date
Not enough to be perfect
Just enough to be who you are
And no one else
Amidst the sea of faces
The sea of shapes
You are an integral part of
As you go on your way
In this universe
Down the street

POEM

We are all made up of others—
             father and mother
only begin it. Teachers and
fellow students, odd
                fugitive companions
of a day, an afternoon, a minute—all
are called into the blend
of oneself.

My daughter sits on my lap
close to our wood stove.
I rub her four-year-old back.
Already she is a puzzle
of herself—a voice that echoes
her friends' voices.

We are all members of one
another, friend and enemy
combined, and not even
death can take the identity
of one from another still alive.
Creation is a tapestry,
a mandala, of ourselves.

We move, and it all moves.

POEM WRITTEN DOWN IN THE DARK

I lie in bed
listening to the dogs bark,
a cold holding my
right ear in
some kind of grip.

You asleep,
Strawberry in her
sleeping bag on
my right,
Cream in her little
bed on your left.

A family...
and I've just put the cats out
finding them cuddled too
close to Cream
not to wake her
one of these minutes.

They're out on the roof now,
looking in from time
to time
at their mysterious
owners.
I cough and blow
my nose;
you stir to the other
side of the bed...

A dog howls,
frogs croak—

there is a thickness
to the earth
—to life—
so much is here.

We strain
to keep our bills
paid, to make
our way up the ladder
of success, but
what is here is here
now, no less
than when we are millionaires.

I'm glad I'm a poet.
It's not a job,
but a calling—whatever
made me go downstairs
naked for the
pad and the pen,
keeping the universe
in motion.

Now it's quiet
but for a lone
cricket.

No better than that—
no more or less
than a man awake
when he should be
asleep in a
rich night, listening
to his child breathing
beside him, not
ready for sleep.

THE GREAT AMERICAN NOVEL

I don't want to write the great American novel
And set people walking across the pages of a book
Doing things like sweating on page 4, praying on page 45,
Making love on 200, and smoking cigarettes on 85, 107,
    136
And a lot of other pages—what good would that do?

What good would it do to make up a hero who combined
All of my good qualities and only a few of my faults
And set him loose through sentences and paragraphs,
Periods and semicolons, as well as continuous commas,
Making the world an arresting drama of keen insights

And killer instincts, of loners and lovers, devils
And angels, the power-mad and the happy poor?
After all, the world is something else when you get
Right down to it: a ladybug, for instance. A child
Who needs her shoe tied. And I don't know if I could

Find the proper time and place for such reality in
My sweeping saga of will and deception, telephone calls
And unbelievable tension, plus booze, pot, and pills.
Would any of my characters be able to stomach, or even
Notice the small tragedy of the leaves in the fall,

A sidewalk chalk drawing, or a Mickey Mouse watch?
Probably not. They would be so obsessed with money and
    war,
The price of oil and the rise of Third World powers that
There just wouldn't be time for such trivia. And my hero
Himself would be lost to me forever, and I would be lonely.

MARRIAGE

Marriage knits our lives
Into patterns beyond
Our natures separately
We go together

Into new worlds of color
And design, I see
What I have never seen
In your steadfast presence

We learn the other's ways
And see our own changed
In reflection, growing
More independent as

We deepen into
Transparent beings,
Seeing our children
So transparently alive.

A DAISY

for Robert Creeley

The sun is shining
The stars are in their places
On the other side of the world

It's heaven to smell the day
Even with a chain saw in the vicinity
The self still half-asleep

Within the body, as quiet as a sponge
And as absorbent
But what made any of us fall for machines

As loud as this one is
Ah, mankind with its toehold
In the universe, yet so bold

To rule a whole planet
With governments of various degrees
Run by various leaders

So hard to get along with even one
Among the tumultuous millions of ourselves
This time it's going to be different

If we can listen to the women
And to the children
And to the trees

The smell of the day
As unimpeachable
As our greatest leader, a daisy

THESE ARE THE DAYS

These are the days
When a small child's face
Is like a blessing on a father's eye

And when his mind accepts
With honest wonder the knowledge
That we grow, grow and die

The tides that take us make us over
Faster than we can control
A life gets out of hand

Only to find itself, surprised
In this or that meadow, city, state of mind
We come to know our own bones

By where they take us
By where they want to go
And finding our own companion

The next thing we know
Is the nature of the children
Following in our wake

Like a number of walking roses, say
Or talking to one another
You hear another's way, not your own

And it is all going on again
And you are not even very old
Just enough to see it coming

MY FATHER'S FLIGHT

for my father's sixty-seventh birthday,
August 31, 1975

My father wrote circles around
The other writers of his day
And still does

He knows it's not just a matter of form
Nor just a matter of content either
It's a matter of both

A lot of people got confused
And they still do
Going back to Gertrude Stein for confirmation

For this or that deep-end they've gone off
Forgetting that Gertrude herself went off *all* of them
And ended up in the middle of the pool

Only because she knew how to swim
My father knew how to fly by the time he was twenty-six
And he's been flying ever since

He flies through short stories, essays, poems
Plays and novels
As well as whatever else he writes

It's all a matter of stamina and delight
In being alive in such a crazy world
He has never been a sentimental writer

But some other writers have called him that
Because he insists on reaching for delight
Even in our time

When delight is apparently unpopular
He's never been a surrealist either
Because surrealism is so unrealistic

Who ever saw a melting clock, for instance
Except Salvador Dali
And even Dali admits he's crazy

Nor has my father ever gone in for the super-macho
Hemingway type of self-presentation
This was taking the importance of being Ernest too far

He thought
And he has never retreated into the folds of self-
Lessness of Mr. J. D. Salinger, the one who got away

Holden Caulfield would probably have harsh words
For his creator, if he could see him now
Staring at the Glasses of his own mind

Oh well, my Dad has gone on
Refining his celebration into the fine energy
Of an experienced man still physically intact

As for Norman Mailer
He has done well considering his weakness
For ideas, hasn't he?

But does anyone read a writer who talks so much?
And Truman C., well he really should be given
His own TV series, no?

And Gore Vidal could be his second banana
Who who would sponsor it:
Ultra-Bright?

John Updike is awfully good too
But of all of them only F. Scott Fitzgerald
Really knew

That it is the quality of the feeling that endures
As Ezra Pound said
And Scott got hung up with a woman named Zelda

Pop got hung up too
But he survived it
He survived his own anger, his own terror

His own madness
And he did it without psychoanalysis
What an example

He did it by writing, celebrating
And discipline, editing
And being older and wiser every day

And now he is sixty-seven
And he is one of the best poets who has ever sung in prose
And he is still flying on the trapeze

Of his own human time
Living proof
That it's the singer not the song

LOVE

The beauty of a summer evening...
The television on in the living room: The Waltons.
A book I like out there too.
But I sneak away to catch the day fading
Into the first minutes of the night.

To be a survivor of all this richness
And to live on, cherishing life, for its own sake.
Singing praises to its light and its night,
The pungency of color in a child's face,
The birth of ideas in the mind.

Outside the fog closes the scene in—
Pale mists the trees move behind.
Closer, the daisy bush just outside this window
Is immobile—the crowd of flowers
Stopped in windless color.

Empty, empty, as I am now—
As I always feared before but now merely notice.
I am time, not space; time to engage
In conversation, gentle interaction, with space.
To make love with the sure touch of time's favor.

No rush, no necessity to be finished—
An understanding with the world of pleasure
That is time itself—the pressure of a hand
Just so, no more the man than the woman,
And no more one another than love.

O MY GENERATION

I

O my generation
        Faster than a speeding bullet
        More like the blinking of an eye
        Or a shadow on the grass
        Ah, the dark clouds, the rain
        Followed by the sun in bloom

O my generation
        A bowl of Corn Flakes, Rice Krispies
        Or on cold mornings Cream of Wheat
        Innocent in our school clothes
        America in Korea, numbers and letters
        How do I write my name?

O my generation
        The softness of a spring breeze
        The ease of birds singing in daylight
        A cowboy picture on TV, a cowboy outfit
        To get all dressed up in, chaps and spurs
        To make another meaning of oneself

O my generation
        We were so young and innocent
        Just like children now, just like children always
        And then came the locomotive
        And then came the mathematics
        And then came the endless chatter

O my generation
        With a magnifying glass and a gum wrapper

With a piece of paper and a comb
With a bicycle, some playing cards, and
clothespins
With a slingshot, a bow & arrow, a BB gun
O my generation, with pick-up-sticks

O my generation
With windows & doors, and patios
Swimming pools and gymnasiums
I.D. bracelets and comic books
O my generation and movie magazines
Confidential, Police Gazette, Gypsy Rose Lee

O my generation
And bus stops, shoeshine parlors
Movie houses and nightmares
O my generation and Mr. Sandman
Tea for Two, Martin and Lewis, Perry Como
O my generation and The Hit Parade

O my generation
And Debbie and Eddie, and Bob and Natalie
"I Like Ike" buttons, alleys and boredom
O my generation and Dragnet
Black and white television, hopeless cases
A deck of playing cards & Marilyn Monroe

O my generation
Flying a kite, riding a bicycle
Watching the light fail as we played before dinner
O my generation and the promise of love
A beautiful girl from school on the elevator
Headlocks and hammerlocks, ducktails and pants
real low

O my generation
    Fist-fights, and feel-ups, neckties and report cards
    O my generation and strange teachers
    O my generation and being sent to the principal's
        office
    Full of terror, full of stories
    And the principal one more harassed man only

O my generation
    And the strange smell of other people's houses
    A feeling like falling off the world
    O my generation and shy first friendships
    Indian wrestling, playing catch
    O my generation and the Soap Box Derby

O my generation
    We grew up so fast, and yet we don't know
    O my generation in locker rooms and coffee shops
    And walking downtown and uptown
    And o my generation and sincerity
    And beauty and truth, sex and love

II

O my generation
    We were barely out of the gate
    We were hardly out of the nest
    We were still children really
    We didn't know what hit us

O my generation
    Smoking marijuana and not even getting high
    O my generation, finally getting high
    Everything definite and funny, cracking up
        laughing

While reading the menu, the range of choices and
    prices
Cosmically disorienting, I'll have pea soup

O my generation
    A snow storm of speed, a shot in the bathroom
    And a rearranged living room, who was that guy
    Anyway, o my generation, time melting in rooms
    All over America while Vietnam exploded
    O my generation the grammar the syntax gone

O my generation
    Our eyes too open, too vulnerable, too full of
        chemicals
    O my generation at midnight at Winterland
    At the Fillmore, at Max's Kansas City
    O my generation and Dylan, the Shakespeare of
        the Sixties
    O my generation and Andy, the Rembrandt of
        Now

O my generation
    And Allen Ginsberg weeping on the Lower East
        Side
    And Gary Snyder honing his craft in a monastery
    And Philip Whalen, a jolly Buddha
    And Jack Kerouac with a red neck to disguise
    His own difficult rainbow

O my generation
    With Jimi and Janis and Jim Morrison
    So quickly they were gone
    Leaving us the open book of their lives
    If we could read between the lines
    And the music like red, green, yellow, and blue

O my generation
     A piece of soot in our eye
     Our brains soft with time departed into
     Bright rooms of incense, dim rooms of incense
     A retinal circus on the subway
     A whole lifetime in the way a man walks

O my generation
     With all the doors open
     With the windows lifted wide
     With a whole new system
     O my generation with our arms spread too wide
     O my generation ready for evil

O my generation
     Then the evil did arrive
     O my generation and Lancelot and Groovy on
          the Lower East Side
     O my generation and the Chicago Convention of
          Life spilling its blood
     O my generation and Manson's caravan demon-
          strating for Evil like a Washington lobby
     O my generation and the other look in our eye

O my generation
     And the strangeness and the fright
     O my generation and a different way of life
     O my generation back on the drawing board
     O my generation sick at heart
     O my generation looking for a new way out

O my generation
     Going off by itself, without farewell
     O my generation feeling like a bit of fresh air
     O my generation reading a book for the first time
          in years

O my generation suddenly silently crying
O my generation with a gentle hand on its own
    face

III

O my generation
    We were too young for the Beats
    Not quite young enough for the Flower Powers
    We were adolescents with Hemingway and
        Fitzgerald
    Adults with Abbie and Jerry
    But not quite any of them

O my generation
    We were too quickly ourselves
    Not to be casualties of the blind spots in our
        makeups
    O my generation and Women's Liberation
    O my generation and getting married
    O my generation and natural childbirth

O my generation
    A little baby is an awesome event
    A new kind of experience
    Every minute taken up, no time for conflict
    O my generation turning the corner of life
    O my generation a mother and a father

O my generation
    It happened so fast
    We weren't ready for this, we couldn't do it
        together
    O my generation and single mothers and
    Single fathers, the children hauling us
    Back into time, pushing space aside

O my generation
> A child's first words, uttered with all its nervous
> system
> O my generation remembering itself so young
> O my generation with sudden sympathy for our
> parents
> O my generation doing a difficult job
> O my generation trying to find clean air for the
> child to breathe

O my generation
> And Welfare, because if you have a child and no
> money you qualify
> O my generation a better way of life every first of
> the month
> O my generation and food stamps, three big
> boxes at the Coop, all organic
> O my generation gardening
> O my generation fixing a hole in the roof

O my generation
> And Jesus, and the *I Ching,* and the stars at night
> O my generation and a rooster at dawn
> O my generation and the old-timers, with years of
> experience in their voices
> O my generation and admiration for the survivors
> O my generation and flowers in the house

O my generation
> And silence at the end of the day
> And the body tired from the hundred stops and
> starts
> O my generation and the phases of the moon
> O my generation and neighbors
> O my generation and exercise and diet

O my generation
>The trees are forever in motion rooted in the
>>earth
>The rain comes down
>Then evaporates into the air again through the
>>leaves
>O my generation and spring water, rain water,
>>well water, water from the creek
>O my generation the night air so fine

O my generation
>The time almost disappeared
>We shortened our names, let our hair grow
>And knew each other by our clothes
>But we couldn't live for very long inside that
>>perfect dream
>Our life kept interrupting us

O my generation
>We are going home into the numbers of the earth
>We have arrived back into minutes and hours
>Days and weeks, months and years
>Time couldn't forget us even in the Eternal
>>Present
>We are arriving back into life

O my generation
>It's time to hold on with all our might
>But it may be easier than we think
>After all, this is the way it goes
>A child blows a bubble and asks you to come and
>>see
>And the cat is also hungry

SNOW IN CALIFORNIA

My daughter's enterprising little spirit
Bestows its gift upon the virgin air:

What excitement the whiteness makes in her!
She clasps it in her mittens

Until it's a snowball which she doesn't throw,
But lingers over, having never before held snow.

Summer Rain

DOMESTIC SCENE

A child plays in a room
in a house in the country;
she hums to herself
as she puts pieces of a building toy
together.

A man sits in the room
with the child,
writing a poem in a yellow tablet,
hoping to have something
to say of the child, himself, the world ...

The little girl begins
to talk to an imaginary friend
she has named "Tra-la";
she talks quite harshly
to this invisible companion,
telling it what it can and cannot do.

The man writing the poem
is rather tired;
he is thirty-two and it is July,
the evening of an active day—
yet he wants to put down something
as the child plays.
"If only I could get the moon into this,"
he thinks.

The little girl is humming, then talking—
"You can do it if you want," she says—
then humming again;
she is busy and unselfconscious,

not quite three years old.

The man is her father
and looks at her with love
for the already clear intricacy
of her character;
she is one who will never be taught
or told anything
but with affection.

Otherwise, she will cry now
and bring the world down to the earth
of her feelings,
the flowerbed of her little soul;
and she is no fool,
the man knows,
and very brave.

Outside—"quiet music," the little girl
suddenly says—two eucalyptus trees
appear absolutely still to the man's eyes;
the day is overcast
in a way typical of the climate of the place.

Quite soon,
in another part of the house,
the man's wife and his older daughter
will wake from their naps,
and the household will quicken
with the activity of getting dinner.

Meanwhile the man is
almost finished with his poem
and the little girl crosses
the room to him
with something she has completed

out of the building toy.

"Isn't it beautiful," she says;
he smiles and nods and says "Yes."

FOR ARMENAK SAROYAN, MY GRANDFATHER

At thirty-six, the story goes,
In the summer heat of Fresno,
You were carried into the house
And placed on a sofa
From which you never rose—

How, stricken in your appendix,
You begged your wife for water
Until she could withhold it no longer;
And when you drank it, your appendix
Burst and you died—

Leaving behind you your wife and four kids,
The youngest of whom, my father,
Would never completely forgive you,
Since his life was split wide open
In a home for orphans at three.

All these years, I have looked at you
From the three or four photographs that remain—
Your open-eyed, almost deer-like,
Yet somehow blunted look,
As if your eyes had only frozen open ...

What could you be thinking?
And didn't you look a little like me?
Well, I am nearly thirty-three now,
And last night I thought I saw clearly
That you had become yourself—

And come to the new world
Wanting only to affirm your discovery.

You were no longer the youth
For whom experiment is a pattern
Of growth; you wanted to repeat

The path you had broken through:
A Christian, a minister with a command of English
That landed you a parish in Paterson, New Jersey,
Under a man named William Stonehill,
For whom you named my father

After you had been tricked into Fresno,
Promised a comparable parish
That never materialized.
Your wife's family was settled in this vineyard country
Because it was something like what they had known at
        home.

But they were not you,
Nor you them;
And when you took up chicken farming
You had already put away what you knew to be
Best in yourself.

You were asked to die again
Just when you knew who you were:
I can see you in my own thirties,
Here in America,
My father having survived the shock

Of your departure,
And I the shock of my father's
Fierce momentum, a reaction to your
Absence: you were the wrong age
For the new world—

I can forgive you.

THE MIND IS A MEDIUM

The mind is a medium
And delights in its own movement,
Disclosures, gestures.

It has a style
For every man, woman, and child;
An alphabet of forms that is

Literally
Inexhaustible. What could not be seen
Within the mind's roving, restless

Eye? An expressionist
As deep as Van Gogh; a minimalism
That contracts

And expands into multiples of its
Own perfect
Nothingness: this mind is pastel

At times,
Chiaroscuro in other, fiercer
Moments, and can be reduced to

The raging
Scribbles of a forlorn child.
But this mind is a stylist, too.

Its view, a river;
Or a knife and fork
To proportion any meal

Set before it. Or else
The laughing mind,
Letting rhythm loosen

Its sphere into
Comedies of manners,
Mores, Mondays, and moths.

An alliterative wonderer,
A wanderer of summer
Mornings, alluded to moods of

Remembered con-
Versations with a plant? What will it
Not go through to sustain

The rapid answering, the listless
Inquiring—a chemical circus
In the extreme;

And yet
The deepest, clearest pool
This mind also is;

As if it had been cosmically
Checked, righted like a tie
In a mirror: a God's eye view

Of itself in the cosmos.

SONNET (IN SCORPIO)

Death makes life divine
Making fluid of the mind
When the mind would carve itself
Some immortal shrine
No weather could ever betray
Yet death does betray it
In the mind, letting in the fluid
That is time—in which only death
Is immortal, only death is in stone
It edges every known thing
With impermanence—indefinite
And *infinite* because fleeting
Touched by death in its own shining now
Eternal death makes life divine

WHEN THE HEART MELTS

When the heart melts
The trees are loving gestures
Graced by moon

When the heart melts
A child's eye
Seems to decorate the town

When the heart melts
Teenagers
Become beautiful

When the heart melts
There is an air of love
Filling the throat

When the heart melts
It is impossible
Not to agree

When the heart melts
The television is divine
And so is the telephone

When the heart melts
The wood stove performs
A service of heat

When the heart melts
Chagall is the dreamer
Asleep in the mind

When the heart melts
Everybody seems to wake up
At the same time

When the heart melts
We go deeper and deeper
Into the feeling

When the heart melts
A song is released
Through the body

SONNET

I sing the subtle beauty of man
And woman, children, and their home
That creature not quite a rose, nor yet a thorn
Born of days stitched in bright use
From dawn to midnight blessed with chores
And encores of dreams of deep inconsequence
Yet filled with a music of the heart's tolerance
Ah, we are creatures, and God blesses us all
With mouths and eyes, and brains to think and pray
And a child's delicate drawing easily finds its way
As an adult, watching, finds his or hers too
Don't think or look too hard, dear worker,
But be with time the partner of a dance
And what follows capture with quick and loving glance.

THE TRANSPARENT MAN

for Freddie Prinze, in Memoriam

You were transparent
The bright shifts in your soft face
And all your vocal expertise
The shticks with which you outwitted time
With a goofy Puerto Rican–Hungarian smile
That made us see you all the way through
To the first primal spark of man
The one who invented fire by going at it
Like nobody's business with a couple of rocks
Or sticks—a real world-beater you were
Chico to the Man who looked up, ravaged
By the whole Western gas-station of his life
Old and wise to every angle that had ever come down the
    pike
Yet you gave him another answer—a soft twinkle in
Your eye that moved him past his desperation
And brought him to the unfamiliar presence of his own
    human heart
Who is this person? To call love out of an old
Song-and-dance man like Ed Brown with
Jack Albertson's seasoned timing, a real survivor,
A real professional over sixty years old?

Chico, Freddie, you were transparent
A stand-up comedian at the approach
Of the brothers on the block who would either laugh or
    fight
Depending on your act—you knocked 'em dead
In Hell's Kitchen before you turned to the New York clubs
Where you worked for free for a while

And if you got a bathroom pass at the High School of
    Performing Arts
They say half the class followed to see you do ten minutes
You had it down to a fine art still in your teens
No money in your jeans, but the unstoppable, cosmic
American winner coming along in your nervous system
In order to shake hands with a delighted (as only by a new
    talent) Johnny Carson
An overnight sensation, Freddie Prinze

You did it, out of the slum and into the Catskills
And then into a TV series where nobody could believe
You were walking around like you were, transparent,
In tight pants, "the mutant Prince," Paul Williams
Called you, because you really were so young and full
Of the soft charm of a young man trying a first mustache
Yet, still, should anyone forget, a seasoned pro
Who knew how to work any house because you'd already
    done it
Then success, dating Raquel Welch—
But a year more and you would be married, with a baby,
And just hitting the hard time of unlocking the parts
You had kept on ice to make your get-away
And you let a bullet fly through your brain in the midst of
    your first try

No one was there to tell you how hard it was
To be where you were and not locked out of every day
The hours and minutes, the sunlight and trees
Of the real world even in Beverly Hills, transparent
Yet your invention nonetheless turned on you
Until you wanted it to end, picked up for wobbly driving
On downs, and still up for the Carter Inaugural Eve
But your face tighter, you were losing that baby fat
And, finally, sort of coasting, weren't you?
Through this high moment of your career

Ah, Freddie, you are clear as myself to me
Calling your manager, your estranged wife, your parents
To tell them you needed somebody to take care of you
You are clear as anyone I've ever known
You are the same person, crying on the roller coaster
Suddenly for real, and the only way off through the soft
    underside of your professional heart
You wanted to get off because you'd been on too long
For a man only twenty-two, and nobody knew what to tell
    you
You wanted them to love you when you were going to be
    more transparent than you were supposed to be
What could they tell you in the midst of your career
And so you shot clear of your career
Transparent

POEM

What makes my little son try
To raise his head and eyes,
To straighten his spine upright
And take a step for all mankind—

Oh, it pushes through him ceaselessly,
The stuff of such strong effort.
With all the will in the world, it thrusts up
Through his nervous system and makes him cry and sing.

And I look into his face, still so delicate
With a newborn's silken transparency,
And see all the answers of his ancestry,
Of my wife's and mine, declaring themselves anew.

And then, suddenly, he is smiling
The complete and unutterable smile
Of one who has neither years nor speech;
And I kiss his ear and smell it.

SPRING

The beauty of a tree
in spring
the first white blossoms
of the plum
aglow in the sunlight

The crisp reach
of its thin branches upward
into a heaven it creates
of its own
delicate fortitude

HOW TO BE AN AMERICAN POET

The secret of poetry is to start simple
And remain simple
All the way through. Oh, there will be those
Who will say this is not true—that the times
Demand a more complicated poetry, full of tiny
Motors which operate fans which blow colorful
Scarves & handkerchiefs, flags & pennants through
The landscape of the poem.

Or something even more refined & magical:
Like pulling a live rabbit
Out of a hat. There are poets who appear only in
Tuxedos, and produce a syntax full of bow-ties
And flashlights. Then there is one whose brain
Has become a diamond, incredible, luminous,
Refracting the light of an intricate city into
The teleprompters of outer space.

There are a good deal of science fiction poets,
Those who ride the rocket ships of extraordinary
Thoughts, made up of equal parts of language and
Language, who disappear into rare verbal con-
Stellations which send chills down the spines
Of innocent readers in the rare book rooms of
Minneapolis, Detroit, Denver, and Berkeley, California.
Joy is a thing with feathers in these poems, and spreads
As smoothly as the NBC peacock used to do.

Moreover, you have a select group who see the comma
As the way in, and out, of all poetic reality. Such
Poems, hunched with the determination to forge an
Electric pattern through plain talk, sometimes de-

Light the mind into déjà-vus, or cause electric storms
In the living rooms of the brain. The heart's telephone
Goes on ringing though, and there is no one to answer
The call. Not the baby nor the kids nor the Mommy

Nor the Daddy nor the neighbors nor the whole town
In the full moon of Grandfather Night. But the next
Morning the birds begin on time, and this is what we
Must remember, what we must hold on to in the terrible
Disorder of our century, the madnesses and absolutes—
Those birds are simple. And being simple, they are
Naturally excellent poets. Sometimes you get to listen
To those morning birds in the intricacies of Shakespeare

Which never lose the spanking freshness of a new set
Of sheets, or silver. As real as a real street corner
Or a rose with the morning dew on it, shaky. Or
Shelley who spoke with the purity of a summer rain
And told us what the trees were, and a person
Among them. Byron, with a heart full of blood and
A limping stride, who had an enormous commercial
        success
Because everyone knew he gave himself whole to poetry.

And they all thought about America, and wondered what it
Might do, what song would follow out of such a vast un-
Known, though the Indians knew it, as the black slaves
Had once known Africa, deep in their nervous systems,
As right as rain, as clear as day. And Whitman made
Himself an instrument equal to such a vast song
And bellowed through the loneliness of the Civil War,
Looking to Lincoln and the sky and his

Fellow mammals amidst the accidents and disasters of
His time. And the all-in-one, one-in-all Walt created
The original mountain spring of our living verse. He

Named it by naming his world, a thing at a time, in
The clear enumerations of his eye. And our poets have
Loved lists ever since, gloating over our variety as
A parent over his children's different eyes. In the
Deep sleep of the 1950s, Allen Ginsberg, a young man

Who had corresponded with William Carlos Williams
And constructed small poems with impeccable personal
Honesty, suddenly struck the golden chord of Whitman's
Primal American voice and gave us *Howl* with the same
Force as a Plains Indian power vision, reuniting us
With ourselves in the industrial excavation of our
Souls which we had been sold along with houses, cars,
And televisions. This voice echoed throughout our planet

And the Beat Generation spawned the Beatlemania of
The sixties, in which a new generation willed
Their time to a standstill in a psychedelic purge
Of intentions and stared into the mandala of their
DNA, while America televised its foot on the moon.
But we have come back from our space odysseys to look
At the violated innocence of our planet's body, and
The American poet must save the actual earth of his own
        voice.

with thanks to Joel Oppenheimer

UP IN THE LOFT

Sitting in the sleeping loft
With six-months-old Armenak
Everything is so clear through the open window
A sunny April afternoon in the meadow
Yellow, green, grayish browns—alive out there

As I am—we are—in here
A minute ago my mind stuck on my ego
Like a fish on a hook
Amidst the wide-open ocean of all this
Which I got a penetrating glimpse of just then through the
    window

And I went out like a light
In a tiny room
And discovered that the building didn't exist
I was actually here
Greater than finding money on the street

My little boy can't talk
Loves to play with his toes
And knows his way around all the nothing
That is and is and is
He and I keep each other company

I toss him around
And feed him his bottle
The birds are going on about something
He sighs
And clucks and smiles and kicks

Shits and pisses on a diaper I've laid out under him

Luckily
For a while he just breathes
And we look at each other
While the eucalyptus trees wave across the meadow

SONNET

I remember the evenings I played as a boy,
Suffused with this same disappearing sunlight,
As dinner is finished just in time to catch
A half hour or more still left to play—my friends' faces
    outside
Settled in their own familiarities—I said goodbye
To the family table to keep the last appointments
Of the day—just the way my two daughters do
This evening, while my son remains in his high chair,
Breathing and carefully examining some french bread,
Sliced, buttered, and left behind by one of his sisters
The world is almost at a standstill—so quiet only
The spoon on the soup bowl speaks, when a horse in the
    distance
Neighs and neighs again—and the only thing left
Is the empty, almost different world before dark

FOR GAILYN

I have loved you,
not as I would,
but as a man
fumbling for answers
in the empty pocket
of himself.

Yet I have seen
the light of a million years
playing through the soft yellow curls
about your ears—swift as lightning,
without words,
seen the truth.

This morning
in a dream
Elizabeth Barrett Browning
spoke a poem to me, standing with her
in the corner of a restaurant
in New York City,

and my grief rose
in an instant
when I caught
the melody she had so
contained through the torn
curtain of her time.

"The pain is gone
in the time
it was, when your arms
were oars

upon the sky ..."—
a poem to a man sitting

at a table
just down
from where we stood.
Her body seemed taut
and fragile
as a vase, holding

aloft
the flowers of her
timeless time.
The man, catching
a few words, moved
his chair and looked

up, an old lover,
politely smiling.
And so have I
sometimes
looked at you:

your steadfast fire
was more
than I could
make an answer
for ... yet I saw.

THE HOUSE

for My Father

The house is like a parent,
Surrounding us with care.
The roof won't admit rain
On a dark day—Strawberry, Cream, & Armenak
At play in the living room
Under the white paper lantern,
Enclosing electric light.

There are corners to it,
Places to snuggle into, as a child finds
In a parent's large embrace—
So large, it encloses all our lives
And provides an interior from which to feel
What is outside.

The birds' intricate messages
On a summer Sunday go on and off
As the water is turned on and off
In the bathroom. A fly
Buzzes through the back room,
As the cat, Chocolate, passes
In the pantry toward the back door.

The sun is shining
On the porch, and the voices of children
Echo in the meadow momentarily—
A whoop, a laugh.
The sudden warmth of the sun is
Like a new, vaster room
Where things have smells.

I am here—with my complications,
And devotions. My mind
Is like the house now, with its familiar
Rooms—accepting me, as I have accepted
Each. Difficult, comfortable ...

I know the kinks and crimps,
The slow leaks and faulty structures
That make up the somehow organic whole of it—
House, mind.
I carry the hammer and nails here and there
For patchwork, and keep an eye on my thoughts.

At 3 A.M. last night, the near full moon
Shining through the living room skylight,
I held sleepless Armenak over my shoulder
And walked him around the moonlit living room:
His mind, my mind, the house, and the sky ...

ADVICE TO A YOUNG POET

Now is your time. The sky in you is equal to the sky above you. Let your nickels and dimes fall into the clear blue lake. Your pockets are full: the springs and pulleys of the universe are at work everywhere, within and without you, like a blossom in spring. Nothing can come between you and the anniversary of being in everything. You are a mirror with eyes and nose, mouth and hair, teeth and a room. Your neighbors are warm with greetings, though troubled by independent lives. They know you are a poet and they want your own wish to be given out of the air of themselves.

Breathe it in. Let each breath contain its myriad vibrations of life: portraits, and empty rooms, reports to rare commissioners in the offices of clouds. You are double, a breathing cartoon of life and humor on the way. You are the highway of this funny poem, your life. Let your arms and legs, torso and mind, maintain a kind of bounce: a kind of tender equivocation in the moment of all things. This is, after all, what poetry is.

Do not be taken in by your own genius. It shouts, perhaps, but your gift is to sing. Oh, no doubt, you must test the bright corridors of death's other side, the extreme ideas that give a name to this and that blanket of the self, cushion of the mind, pillow of the heart. You are almost too young to feel, except generally, an overall wellness of the heart, the luck of your kind to be alive in the first place.

This is real. Trust it. Make homages, medallions, merit badges, monuments, notes, cities, extravaganzas, Broadways, honors, wastebaskets, and apples, of such insinuations. You will be regarded as innocent in mind only—the love of what this is will be held steadily in the daily returns of life, as if the universe had multiplied your own poem. The feet will have this spring, although it isn't necessary for you to notice at all.

Beware of any too pointed attention: your brain is so little in the making of this bargain. The harsh realities of your error are as rubber the soul tests, and tests again—but growing is too enormous to disturb by the pollutions of the self. Let love be the dance of the cells, and the beloved in the exact movements of the dance. You are one with the actual quality of light: in autumn, red.

WINTER MIDNIGHT

after reading Michael McClure

Can I let the winter go without a poem?
Let the minutes disappear wordlessly
As the moon is gone by morning. And yet
It returns. I've seen winter enough times
By now to know it comes again. I am myself
The winter as it enters me, changes the complexion
Of the blood, turns my thoughts deep into themselves.

Why write a poem to commemorate this cycle
That is as much of what I am as my arm, or
The moon. I don't get enough facts into my poems.
This year I saw racoons in the moonlight,
Playing with the abandon of creatures utterly
Untroubled by abstractions. They had come for our
Chickens, who sat inside their coop in a continual
Perplexity, almost human, seemingly sleepless

While the racoons, two little ones with a family foursome,
Wrestled on the lawn. The planet is set up for
Wild things, not money and reputations, not desks
And questions, but the obliterating intelligence of
Pure play. The mind indistinguishable from its own
Body, like the mind of a poplar, which is pure shape, mobile
Upon the air. There is no way to make a living as a poet
In America, and yet I often make some kind of meal

Of a poem. I see the light, the radiant suffusions
Of this world and I want a kind of geometric song
To speak of it, to say it—so it will be in speech too.
Like snow falling, like snow falling, like snow falling.

SONNET

As I watch my daughters' faces climb through time
And my little son grow into talk
I realize this is the gift, the great reward that I sought
The rock I found at the center of my dream
With everybody's initials carved on it
Something hard to understand in language
Yet actual as the blades of grass, the roses climbing the
      fence
Or the cricket's repeated opinion of the earth
As I see my children look closely into my eyes
And notice them noticing me noticing them
While the clock is ticking and everything is just as
      important
As it was two hours ago—and yet I forget then
I forget everything for a second in the pale moment
Of no one at all that makes life great

SONNET

The unutterable sadness of our lives
You and I carried on this inexorable tide
Of minutes, hurtled toward the other side
Through popular songs, and distant lands
Through print and time and the abrupt barking of dogs
One day we will be gone in democracy
As it continues to pursue the equity of what is
Oh, for a moment, you saw it clearly
And I saw it clearly, and our lives mixed in three
Children who even now, asleep in the darkened house
Move further on into identities and cells
And long shots and loves and more of the large dream
We gave them as though it were ours to give
Which it was in a way—like today, like tonight

EVERYTHING IS GOING ABOUT ITS BUSINESS

The plums are ripening
Poets are living in hovels, ecstatic
As living models of what you can do
If you can't do anything else
Children are playing with each other
In modern updated dramas of Mama & Grandma
A little boy stands at the window, watching snow,
And thinking snow, too, through other thoughts
There's a wonderful quality now, suddenly,
To the light on the porch as the moths flutter
And the fragrance in the air is pure and rich
The ocean is going constantly
Along with the highways and the all-night take-out joints
People are getting in accidents, dying, and being saved

LOVE'S BOUNTY

I looked through my love's eye
Into the deepest midnight of time.
It was black as black velvet
With a million stars like scattered diamonds.

•

The pleasure of kissing you
Involves the innocent night
And the transparent stairs of time.
Your lips are pilgrims; our kiss the shrine.

•

And I discovered I was a Persian prince
Leaving fingerprints all over eternity,
Loving you—a white goddess, a smile.

•

I give you my hand
And catch your eyes.

ON BEING A POET

Being a poet has meant something special to me,
That quality which has been almost impossible to describe
Except in a poem, having something to do with grains of
    sand,
Or the endlessness of stars in the night sky,
Or which might also reduce itself to the primacy of a small
    stone.

I always wanted to let this mind become clear in my poems,
Short and long, and to let the reader see beyond I.Q.
Or anything other than the simple shape of being this way.
I tried and to some extent succeeded here and there
But the reward was always the being itself writing the
    poem.

It's interesting, too, because no matter how many changes
    you go through,
From the direct grasp of youth to the more subtle turns of
    middle life—
Which is fuller and slower—the feeling remains
    fundamentally the same—
A oneness with being that cuts across the minutes and the
    miles.
It is an ongoing sense of arrival

No different, really, than being in love, but less specific
In its object of affection. It is like a tantra for each
And every wave and particle of the universe, becoming
The inner and outer being of life. I can feel quietly
The same, everywhere. Fear subsides. Ideas go away.

Ambition becomes a mockery of what is real, for you are

Looking into the eyes of time and space everywhere.
I think I first encountered this feeling riding home
On the 79th Street crosstown bus one night when I was
Going to high school in Manhattan. I was worried about
    school.

I was very much inside my complications. I imagine my
Brow was furrowed, although I was only fifteen or sixteen.
It was already dark outside—it was winter now,
When the light is gone by 4:30 in New York. I was lost
In my life. And then, in an instant, in literally the blinking

Of an eye, I could suddenly see I was on a bus, and see
    through
The bus—as it moved on—into the night outside, and all
    was
Forgotten, all was forgiven, and I was simply alive inside
Of all life. This feeling wasn't ecstasy, exactly. But it
Wasn't less than ecstasy. It was full of deep acceptance,

Inside and outside. I felt, I would say, perfectly OK,
In the most literal sense of those words. There was no
Hope, and no fear. There was nothing other than everything
Itself, filling me, being me, as I was being it. It didn't
Matter about school, because I was truly alive.

And this is the feeling I sometimes have when I want to
    write
A poem. It is usually just a couple of words which
Come into my mind to start me off, but the words seem
To have a weight and body to them, like valuable coins.
They let me know I should sit down and write.

THE OLD ROOSTER'S SOLILOQUY

My son began singing one morning at daybreak
Before I woke, and crowded the coming days with his noise
    and lust.
Dozens of times, I jumped him on top of his mother or
    another.
He wouldn't learn, jumping me instead in the same
    position.

I tried to keep him off the feed in the morning:
Half my size, his mother an Aracana—
But locked up together each dawn I could feel his surge
In my ears, echoing through me like some old legend.

The sun made him proud; I made him strong.
Hating his rude cries and impatience—
What could I do in the red evening?
Facing him down, my life smacked of sunlight and blood.

On Easter morning, he drew away from me,
Reared up his fresh talons, and sharply drew my blood.
I fought him until the two of us stood stiff in our own dried
    blood;
At the end of the day, hobbled with him into the coop.

Three new chicks had been born, probably his own jism.
My own cry at dawn startled me, so shallow and gone;
His own rose up as if he hadn't had half the beating.
And the next week I healed to keep him at bay again.

On Friday, he turned on me once more, and I saw it all
    coming;
Dragged myself under the house, still breathing.

He and the hens were locked up together, I waited out the
    end ...
Past midnight, the racoon pulled me out and my cries

Came out of me from all sides—the night went wild in the
    moonlight.
I was eaten barely alive, yet surprised by such savagery,
    expired
With cries I couldn't have guessed were in me. He must
    have heard.
Now I'm somewhere else inside his startled eyes.

AMERICA

A father
with no father
like my father
before me—

I tread the days
with uncertain
step, amidst my small
son's revelries,

and am amazed,
and have been moved
to tears at the gentleness
of men.

SMALL TOWN

I am a patriot
of these parts
and wear in my face
the faces of the others hereabouts—

I am confused
by such human complicity
into a general elation or sorrow.
Who are we, after all,

But the stray oneness
of ourselves, the fact that we
all die, and inhabit
the sun.

The Moment

THE GOLDFISH BOWL BY MATISSE

I hear the cars
Which I thought last night were airplanes
The cars up on the highway
Now they are cars, last night planes
I thought maybe

Something ticks somewhere on the bed-table
A single tick, like an unclenching
Amidst the internal laws of matter
A clock? A box?
Restless—as I am

For the quietness of being here and there
At the same time
Like the goldfish bowl Matisse painted
The four red goldfish in a bowl
Surrounded by foliage

It took me several weeks
Passing the poster each day
To notice what those colors
At the top of the water were
I kept passing the Matisse

Until I could see he had painted it all
The fish and the reflected fish
Both red gold
No difference in the painting
Between the real and its reflections

FOR PAUL BLACKBURN

The other night
I heard your voice again
That smooth guttural of yours
That seemed to have pebbles in it
Like a dry tide going in and going out

And I wondered if your ghost
Had somehow arrived close by
Your old lessons reviving
In my mind, as they have from time to time
Before and since you died

We never got along
And yet you gave me something
I didn't find among older friends
So strict in your own poetry
You wanted mine larger than I had made it

And told me not to be at home
With what was easy
I didn't agree, went away stung
By what I took to be your parsimony
Agreed when Fee told me what you said was truer of your
          own poetry

Then one night at the bar at the Five Spot
Watching Denise and Diane di Prima read
You put your finger through a hole where my jacket
Had come undone where the sleeve joined the shoulder
And asked me if I didn't have a girlfriend to mend it

"Not at the moment," I replied, cool but angry

And you smiled as if you knew my blank room
Before I had told you—yet closer then
Than you had ever been, smiling
I felt you had seen me

Some years later but before you died
I dreamed that scene again and when you put
Your finger through, I lashed out and beat you down
In the fiercest rage I ever let come through
So that when I heard of your death

I wondered if my dream hadn't help kill you
Alive, I saw you one more time
You sat in back of Gailyn and me
At Ebbe Borregaard's St. Mark's reading
Where you called to him admiringly to "sing!"

I held Gailyn's hand the whole time
To let you see I had found my wife
And at the end of the reading, passing you
You looked up and gave me the kindest nod
That, yes, you had seen

When I finally read *The Cities*, I thought of you
As unique among your peers
You refused to teach or to cultivate the young
Except as equals, you wouldn't prey on
Their admiration, you went your own way

To the end—
And the poems held the strict sorrow
Of your life with a pure lyricism
I could finally, as in the beginning, admire
Your craft, yes, but for song

FOUR POEMS

1: POEM

The mountain is only a while from here
Up from the water
In the night of other lives, cars
That go by outside houses

I've no idea, but the tender music
Of my own night
At last a grownup of some sort
Enough to see where I've been

As what I am, the moonlight
The tunes that cross the stars
And equal the heart
My father and mother one in me

2: FOR MY DAUGHTER STRAWBERRY

At nine, your integrity
Takes me beyond whatever I know of you
You show the shores of some common universe
Sharing thoughts, jokes, puzzled wonderment

How innocent a woman is
Guileless within the feminine miracle
Looking out at the world with its crickets
And phonograph records

194

The saintly innocence of *seeing* anything:
Gone, as you smile at the little brother you have
Lost in the lineaments of his being three
As unique as anything that makes you laugh

3: FOR GAILYN

You do your paintings
Don't worry about me
If the deer get into the garden
We'll make sure it's only in our dreams

I'm going to drift deeper into my vocation
Get a little wilder, having found myself
As you have, what is yours
So there's no trouble going home

I've got a record on, everyone's asleep
I'm not thinking but breathing here
Awake and asleep at the same time
Now that it's night outside

4: ABOUT POETRY

for My Mother

There's nothing to it
Emily Dickinson understood it perfectly alone
Walt Whitman made another version of it
Inserting everything in its mirror

Every few years I've gotten extraordinarily happy
Figuring out a way through my own personality
And just outside it, right at that moment
When I'm nothing but a door, maybe

No hinges even, there's poetry
Your earnest, never literal look
And Pop's exuberant impostures, laughter
I'd forgotten it could just be, nothing

A DREAM

I dreamed I found out
Death was no big deal
No more really
Than a kind of invisible membrane
You walk through
To the other side of the day
The same kind of thing
As lets a mouse know
A person just opened his eyes in the room
In the middle of the night
So the mouse stops making noise
And it was such a relief to know it
I was walking along
And the sun was shining
When it got through to me
And a great weight seemed to lift
From my heart
I felt warm and happy and courageous
As if everything were possible
And the world was a perfect situation

FOR JIM CARROLL

They've discovered a particle
The smallest so far
That has no substance whatsoever
Yet unerringly reflects the charge
Of its opposite number

It's a reflection, then?
A reflection
The beginning of us
And everything? Clusters of reflections
Making up the atom; atoms

Becoming tables and chairs
Voices and dares, a basketball flying
Through the air and into the hoop
Demonstrating the fraternity of matter
As a matter of flair

A kind of telepathy that tells you
Where you are—in midair—
And nothing can go wrong anywhere
Because you're riding a wave
You're meant to be there

THE PAGE

I make myself still
Writing these words

I reach across the page
As if to inscribe the moment

And I'm planted
In the room

The sunlight in the geraniums
At the window

The birds' delicate traceries
In the air around the house

All the announcements
Of the present moment

I am bound to
As I make a partner in space

And we grapple, or coincide
Like dancers, across the page

Moving, yet in being here
One thing

Pen and muscle, ear and mind;
And day inside and outside

The page, all one—
So still

DECLARATION

In my mother's house
I wrote my first poems

And the first of a new decade
twenty years later

Thirty-six years old, listening
to the cars outside

The bed spread with papers
at four A.M. in modern civilization

Searching for the order
that brings courage

The act of attention
brought home in going out of

Itself—joining
the moment of anything

And disappearing
within it

So that the bedrock
is no thing

But union
to the poet

An elusive verb,
the muse herself

And yet in the instant
everything

All these years, the ruins
of the lives spent

Heralding the emptiness
apprehending the whole

Leaves of grass or
a redheaded blackbird

The huge black crow
with serious business

Beside the chicken coop
watchful

For the ground attack of another
meanwhile eating

But the sun rises
on the grown man

The same as on the schoolboy
and the crisis has receded

For the moment
into it

For another nameless bit
of the same thing

That made a million stars
the empty mirror

Of the universe
glimpsed

In the pure gold
of another morning in the world

With its birds
birds

NIGHT FLIGHT

for Robert Bly

My mother, a sorceress, demonstrated
through my own person, flight.
She told me to relax
as much as I could, meanwhile
walking me backwards into
position. I was to land

on a mat at the top of a temple.
Suddenly, I was turning over
in space—
like a backwards high dive—
flying!

The idea of landing repelled me.
I didn't want to come down
and did not meet the mat
to demonstrate to the onlookers
my mother's powers.

Instead I flew like a bat through
the open portals of the temple,
circling down.

I wondered what the sorceress
would make of it
as I came down.

I didn't see her—
but ended up in a room where
a gay man was talking

to the teacher and the three
other students.

Then I woke up.

My daughter, the younger one,
the one like my mother, had
had a nightmare and I went into
her room to comfort her.

I kissed her goodnight
and came back to bed to
write this down, remembering
the joy of flying! My mother's
powers—like what a guru is
said to have shown a disciple.

The favor of the female is necessary
to ascend.
My daughter is crying again.

IN GREECE

as
the
kids

playing
soccer
broke

out
of
the

strict
concentrations
of

their
game
coming

toward
me
haphazardly

across
the
field

in
a
kind

of
free-style
ballet

their
whole
multitude

touched
by
the

evening
sunlight
my

mind
too
broke

free
of
its

usual
densities
and

I
saw
them

dancing
dancing
dancing

GETTING MY CAR REPAIRED

I take the city of San Rafael
    on foot
        the day the Shah of Iran died
I'm back inside
    the lonesome stranger of my youth
        looking at everything twice
I've got nowhere to go
    up all night, my mind rioting
        with a visit from my sister Lucy
Who told me I had the ball rolling now
    and soon the money would come in
        my old pal Lu
who said Pop and she and I
    shared the same sense of humor
        so few understood
And now that we weren't seeing Pop
    we needed each other for laughs at least
        I agreed
seeing her cigarette-edged eyes
    getting brighter and brighter
        in my daughter Strawberry's room
as the morning light rose outside

PHOTOGRAPHING ROCKS AT AGATE BEACH

How these tiny things speak to me
Beside my little son's sneakers
Enormous in the camera's frame
Amidst these lilliputian citizens
Who never speak never sing
But lie in myriad thousands
Along this beach, inviting the eye
Into an infinity of mirrors
The very consonants of time
As two seagulls glide above us
And the secret is multiplied
Everything is alive, even the stillest thing
Touched by a feather in the wind

THE MOMENT

The moment is like this. Suddenly you *see*. The words are gone; the vision is absolutely empty of the usual interior monologue that accompanies our daily round. It might be anything. An oil stain on a rain-soaked pavement. A tree in sunlight. A shoulder; a handkerchief; a tricycle.

Part of the seeing is not knowing what is being seen; not knowing, that is, in the ordinary sense of knowing it by naming it. Instead, one is seeing with a complete attention that transcends the names—exceeds them, outspeeds them.

There it is, suddenly: nothing.

Nothing is misunderstood. It is the name given to what goes beyond simple naming.

Because the seeing here is more than the object seen; the seeing is an action in which the see-er and the seen commingle to the degree of losing one another as separate, discrete identities. They merge, and in merging are one (moving) thing.

This nothing is—and is—and is.

Until the name occurs.

Sweater, say. Or orange.

Stopping it. Giving the name ends the dance: the verb is replaced by a noun.

·

This kind of seeing is beauty, too, perhaps even in the precise sense that Keats meant it in his "Beauty is truth, truth beauty." For in the end might not the beautiful be defined as whatever empties the mind, causing the seeing to become pure, mirror-like?

The act of a mirror is self-dispossession. Consciousness.

·

Lew Welch, speaking of poets, once said that the suicide misses by just a quarter of an inch. What he meant, I think, is that self-dispossession is the source of poetry—but the act of the poet is to die *into* the world, not out of it.

PRAYER

Oh, though I
Know so little
Of night and of day,
Yet may I sing—

Sing of it sweetly;
As I may rise,
My heart resolved
By some dream

That held a key
So I felt everything
Through and through:
A whole neighborhood

Of feeling
Passing through me.
I, in my trousers
And shoes

With coins in my pockets;
What I know of identity:
The moon—
Identity!

AKHMATOVA

Poet, still pool,
Stopping the world
By reflecting,

Say, these
Yellow leaves of the plum tree,
An autumn prayer of color—

Ruffled by surface buzzes,
Croakings,
Sticks and stones...

Yet holding,
In the depths of your embrace,
Silence.

JOHN LENNON, 1940–1980

I wish I could see into
Space and time
And know why John went through

To the other side
While Yoko and Sean and Julian
Are left without him now

And the Beatles will never unite again
Except in Heaven
I wish I knew why John was gone

And how his number could come up
So suddenly like that
And somebody get confused

Like I am you
And we are me
And try and succeed at killing John Lennon

And make little Sean wonder
If the court that decides what to do
With the man who killed his father

Is a basketball court or a tennis court
And later start crying
The day his Dad and his pal John

Went suddenly into a new dimension
Without another word
At the end of the first year of the new decade

And made the whole world
Stop for a moment
To wonder even beyond

The shock and the horror
To wonder how John
Could just be no one

Suddenly
Without a warning
Where there had always been

Such a clear man
Someone we could count on
To be living a life

And going about his business
It makes me wonder what Death is
After all

To come so close to the whole world
By taking away this man we all knew
As if Death were saying something

When it said
John Lennon

THE DOME

My whole life
Is like a dome
I'm walking through
And in the middle of the night
I wake up

Knowing I'm half way
My body's momentum
A man's now
Like a rocket that's steady
Through the ether

Though somehow larger
Not smaller
With its discarded parts
Inside I know a vast
Lumbering si-

Lence
That is the rhythm
Of the creature man
Life has caught
Up with me

At last
As I see
The dome curve
Down way up ahead
At the end

Of this journey
And feel

Within my chest
The nothingness
Which is at once

Knowing I will
One day
Die, and
At the same time
Eternity

BOLINAS

The eucalyptus leaf
falls, twirling

through the dappled
sunlight, everything

changing in its
acrobatic

descent, the light
glancing off one side

and then the other,
all these atoms and

molecules
redistributed,

and I—
immersed in this

spectacle
on my way

downtown through
the grove—make

one more part
of the mosaic.

DAY AND NIGHT

Like a drop
of ink
as it hits

the water—
the whole
glass

going black:
in death
and vision,

decompression—
the soul
united

across
space and
time;

the heart
that was
blind,

a healed thing,
whole.
This

is what
the poet knows
and how he

grows apart.
Oh foolish one,
oblivious

of broken
light:
the one contained

holds the day,
the one apart
the night.

AFTERWORD

1

In late August of 1972, when my wife Gailyn and I and our one-and-a-half-year-old daughter, Strawberry, arrived in Bolinas, I was almost 29 years old and had become known for writing minimal poetry sometimes consisting of a single word. One of these one-word poems, "lighght," was chosen after its appearance in *The Chicago Review* for a National Endowment for the Arts Poetry Award, and was henceforth perennially invoked over the next three decades during any NEA controversy.

The fact was, though, I hadn't really written anything for five years. We'd recently been in London where I could feel myself limbering up for more writing, but any actual writing had been sporadic and—well, minimal. Arriving in Bolinas was what Jung would have characterized as a synchronicity. Everything that had been missing up to now was right in front of me.

A young writer's ego is a delicate matter, subject as it is to routine battery and assault. When I wrote the first section of a long poem called "Lines for My Autobiography" one afternoon on the typewriter in the poet Joanne Kyger's house, where we were staying while Joanne was on the East Coast, I was both exhilarated and uneasy. After all, it was two and a half pages long and I'd never before written a poem of even half its length. I ended up throwing it in the wastebasket, but Gailyn fished it out, read it, and told me it was the best thing I'd ever written and to go on writing it.

The change was of course more than one of simple length. It involved a fundamental redefining of the role of writer from that of artist in a stricter sense—a maker of objects such as my one-word poems, for example—to one who records life as it is lived, and while still alert to artistic opportunities, one who in essence is tuned to a wavelength in which art is secondary to life.

The novelist Edmund White remarked that in the early seventies "an avant-garde of content" spontaneously evolved, and this certainly struck a chord with me. I began speaking as a citizen, as it were, about all the things that were most important to me: my wife, child, family, friends, and community.

What was it that prompted me to break into this new phase? The difference was in no small part in the place itself, Bolinas. With numerous literary colleagues of my generation also residents of the small town at the western edge of Marin County, I was no longer the fish out of water I'd felt like in most other places. When I gave a reading in the town that was attended by these old friends, who emanated uncomplicated approval and support, something extraordinary happened.

When one is given approval of this level, a psychological reordering can take place, and in my case I think it gave me the confidence to speak in a fuller voice from the center of my own life. In the cultural climate of today, in which public support for the arts is considered expendable, one knows that for such a threshold to occur now comprises an even more uncommon grace note.

But what was it about Bolinas, exactly? It was a community in which people of my age and general background and experience were fortuitously empowered, having just empanelled the Utility Board, for instance, after a recall election challenging the installation of a giant sewer system that would have laid the groundwork for runaway expansion and development.

Before I turned thirty, then, I found a place in a

community of some 2,000 people in which the town official-dom was of my own generation. Like me, too, most of them were originally from the East Coast, and I was soon friends with many of them. If it was serendipitous chance that got me there, once I recognized the effect the place had on me psychologically, I tried to make the most of it.

A writer must respond opportunistically to such a situation, after all, because it's not likely to occur often in the course of one's working life. First there must be a place and time in which to write, but given that, the psychic X-factor provided by Bolinas is exactly the sort of lightning one waits to be struck by. In one fell swoop, it provided a new chapter in my writing life and simultaneously engendered an aesthetic that has endured into the present. I laid claim to my own history and experience and also began to address the broader reality of the day. In retrospect, it was the transformation that made me a writer.

2

The economic liabilities of being a poet are of course well-known, and, as one grasps intuitively before understanding it rationally, such liabilities have cultural implications, too. A poet in America, it is universally understood, must be a teacher in order to survive. If one doesn't possess the proper degrees or the appropriate inclination, one looks the problem of survival swiftly in the face. Yet there is also a subterranean tradition in America of the poet as trickster, as a sort of cultural coyote figure who keeps eluding the status quo, even while he/she continues to probe and pierce it.

The figures of the Beat Generation, which preceded and provided impetus for my generation, the generation of the 1960s, modeled this tradition for us vividly. Such figures as Jack Kerouac, Allen Ginsberg, William Burroughs, Gregory Corso and Diane di Prima were spiritual and aesthetic outlaws whose work spoke more directly to us than much of what we found in the cultural mainstream. Perhaps even more importantly their work reflected a lifestyle not otherwise a part of official public consciousness.

Although Allen Ginsberg was the most famous poet of his time, if one were to see him on the street or at a reading or at a party, one could approach him and speak to him. Although Kerouac was a more reclusive figure, I learned when I met him that he practiced the same directness and openness to an even greater degree. The most powerful aspect of such a presence in one's society is also the most implicit, and therefore perhaps the hardest to grasp. These artists were being themselves for us, the succeeding generation, in a larger, fuller, and more humanly rounded way than we had learned to expect.

In essence, they were modeling for us a style of being that was communal as opposed to hierarchical. Although Allen Ginsberg could be misogynist and Jack Kerouac could sound like a redneck, they both communicated in an unofficial, informal, human way that bespoke a deep-seated egalitarianism. An important part of the cultural inheritance of my generation, then, had to do with this ability of our precursors to cut through ingrained patterns and expectations and make themselves known to us in a deeper, more direct way.

In the end, I find I'm describing something close to the traditional role of the poet/artist throughout history. Yet the Beat Generation was like a cultural spore that infected a large part of the succeeding generation, which in turn provided impetus for the cultural and political ferment of the Sixties. If our given society viewed the Sixties generation as an aberration, those of us who chose to carry on the mission as writers clearly had our work cut out for us. After an initial honeymoon period with mainstream publishing, there was a fairly quick lockdown in the literary establishment and one found oneself wondering what was next.

Bolinas was the kind of answer one wouldn't have dared to expect. Since many of the poets I knew had now married and started families, a small town in the country from which a large city was accessible—San Francisco being less than an hour away—was an ideal place to settle. The immediate surroundings were nurturing both socially and environmentally, and the city was nearby for cultural reinforcement.

But the deepest promise of the place had to do with living a life as an integral part of a larger community: with letting go of the trickster/coyote mode imposed on us by the larger society and participating as full-fledged citizens. From this perspective, it was the *next step*, moving the egalitarian model of the Beats from the periphery into the center of the life of a community.

This was the promise of Bolinas, and the one that provides the inspiration for many of the poems I wrote in the first year or so that I lived in the town. For the first time in my writing life, I had my bearings, so to put it. Less than a year after our arrival, I began my first prose book, *The Street: An Autobiographical Novel,* which remembered the Sixties, and it was written with a strong sense that there was a large group of people to whom it could be addressed: those who like me had lived through the Sixties and were now making their way on in life.

One of the pleasures and rewards of a cohesive society is the sense that there is a language common to its members—indeed, the use of that language implicitly evokes that larger group. At the same time, a writer must speak of common experience or risk not being understood. For both Gailyn as a painter and me as a writer, starting a family that would eventually include two more children was a commitment to the common life, and we both, I think, understood it as a decision that would have a profoundly determining impact on our work.

In effect what the Beats had begun to dismantle was the sense of the artist as a specialist that had been an immediate legacy of the post-war Forties and Fifties. Their rebellion against a proprietary style—as purveyed by the New Critics, for example—corresponded to their candor and informality socially. One of the vocational hazards of the artist is the isolation that occurs when one lives at a significant remove from the daily routines of the majority of one's society. Having a family, which the Beats in many cases didn't do, was a way to reinforce that common ground. Even more than our shared pursuit as writers, it was our lot as young parents that brought us together in those early years in Bolinas.

Gary Snyder wrote that he noticed that the rhythms of the work he did at a given time extended into the rhythms of his poetry. The implication that there is work to be done outside of one's art was another important legacy that flew in the face of the cultural norm portrayed in the mainstream media. The artist, again, is encouraged to become a specialist, and to manufacture a product that will feed the economic machine. On the other hand, the idea of a *career* as an artist is, in the deepest sense, a contradiction in terms. One works, after all, not to produce a product but to continue to learn to be the kind of person who can, at the appropriate moment, make a poem or a painting or a passage of music that will speak to one's time. And that of course is a full time job, whatever it is one actually does hour by hour or day by day.

As a writer in Bolinas, I eventually moved from an initial concentration on poetry into prose. As this happened, my poetry became more sporadic, and, I hope, as befits the passage from 28 to 37 years old, deepened. The title poem of this collection, "Day and Night," was also the last I wrote in Bolinas, just a month or so before I got word that my father was dying, and in retrospect it seems to me to be a reflection on his life and the life of the artist in general.

A.S.

Printed November 1998 in Santa Barbara
& Ann Arbor for the Black Sparrow Press by
Mackintosh Typography & Edwards Brothers Inc.
Text set in Plantin by Words Worth.
Design by Barbara Martin.
This first edition is published in paper wrappers;
there are 200 hardcover trade copies;
100 hardcover copies have been numbered &
signed by the author; & 20 copies lettered
A–T have been handbound in boards by
Earle Gray & signed by the author.

Photo by David Mitchell

ARAM SAROYAN was born on September 25, 1943 in New York City. He attended public and private schools on both the East and West coasts and graduated from Trinity School in Manhattan in 1962. After attending the University of Chicago, New York University, and Columbia, he started a literary magazine, *Lines*, in New York in 1964, publishing the work of Charles Olson, William Burroughs, Philip Whalen, Ian Hamilton Finlay, and Ted Berrigan, among others.

His one-word poem "lighght" became the subject of ongoing decades-long government and public debate after being chosen for a National Endowment for the Arts Poetry Award by Robert Duncan in 1968. His poetry has been widely anthologized and appears in many textbooks. Among the other collections of his work are *Aram Saroyan* and *Pages.*.

Saroyan's prose books include *Genesis Angels: The Saga of Lew Welch and the Beat Generation*; *Last Rites*, a book about the death of his father, the playwright and short story writer William Saroyan; *Trio: Oona Chaplin / Carol Matthau / Gloria Vanderbilt—Portrait of an Intimate Friendship*; *The Romantic*, a novel that was a *Los Angeles Times Book Review* Critics' Choice selection; a memoir, *Friends in the World: The Education of a Writer*; and a true crime book, *Rancho Mirage: An American Tragedy of Manners, Madness and Murder*. His first prose book, *The Street*, is being made into a movie. Most recently he has written a series of plays.

A past president of PEN Center USA West, Saroyan is a faculty member of the Masters of Professional Writing Program at USC. The father of three children, he lives in Santa Monica with his wife, the painter Gailyn Saroyan.